2M W

disasters
to
dreams

a gritty guide to finding
SUCCESS
in the face of failure

D1496346

For my mom, who has given so much and asked for so little.
You are my hero.

WILD MONKEY

DisastersToDreams@gmail.com

ISBN: 978-0-578-95454-7 (paperback)

ISBN: 978-0-578-95635-0 (hardback)

ISBN: 978-0-578-95455-4 (ebook)

Ordering Information:

Special discounts are available on quantity purchases by corporations, associations, and others. For details, contact DisastersToDreams@gmail.com

contents

disasters
to
dreams

a gritty guide to finding
SUCCESS
in the face of failure

chris patrick

introduction: a perfect shitstorm

Mike Tyson famously once said, "Everyone has a plan till they get punched in the mouth." But I say that sometimes getting punched in the mouth is the best thing that can happen to you. Not by Mike Tyson, of course, that shit would hurt. By life. Knocked out cold in the fifth round with a bare-knuckled uppercut square to the jaw courtesy of the heavyweight champion of the world. Kicked so hard, right in the cojones, that you see stars beyond the observable universe. A shitstorm on such a grand scale that you have to call in FEMA to clean up the aftermath.

Life hasn't always been easy for me—and I'm sure it hasn't always been easy for you. That's why I've embarked on this fantastic journey. I wanted to share some of my biggest catastrophes—and greatest comebacks—in an effort to help people who may have experienced a serious hardship, traumatic event, or just a general fuck-up, to live their absolute best lives.

But this book isn't about me, this book is about you. Because if I was able to make it through—thriving—I know you can do the same.

I hope this book will inspire and motivate you to live with intention and determination. To realize that not getting what you thought you wanted at the time might turn out to be the best thing that ever happened to you. To discover how a perfect shitstorm can turn your train wrecks into trophies, your failures into fortunes, and your disasters into dreams.

We all have dreams. That's what makes us human. But sometimes those dreams don't come true. Sometimes the hero doesn't get the girl. Sometimes you get dumped on. But within these pages, I will challenge you to see that when you fail to get what you want, you're better off for it.

Which reminds me: if you've made it this far, then I'm guessing you don't mind the occasional use of an expletive if it helps to get a point across. If that's true, then this book is for you. If not, then put it back on the shelf, or better yet, pass it along to someone who *doesn't* give a shit about the casual use of profanity, but *could* use the encouragement and advice that can be found in these pages. I tell it like it is. And sometimes, let's be honest, what IT is, is a total shitshow.

But shit isn't all bad. It has its uses. For example, it's the best fertilizer on the planet. It enriches the soil to better feed plant life, which, in turn, benefits animal life. In other words, shit can actually nourish and help things to grow.

Another great thing it does for us is rid us of waste and toxins.

So, what I'm saying is, when it seems like your life has gone down the toilet, it can actually be the start of something great—if you make it work for you.

I did. And now I'm living what some would call the American Dream. I'm a successful, self-made man living with my beautiful wife and daughter in our new dream home: A far cry from the rebellious, broke-ass, intoxicated, pissed-at-the-world punk rocker of my younger years. But I had to go through some tough shit to get here.

I got here by not allowing the fear of failure or the judgments of others to paralyze me.

I got here by realizing that not getting what you want can actually be an amazing blessing.

Most of all, I got here by being totally true to myself. And you can too.

Acknowledging your history and seeing the truth of it all will help you to better understand your failures for what they truly were: the building blocks toward your future success. And in looking back, you'll find that the times you felt you failed to get what you wanted, you actually *did* end up getting what you wanted as a result—or something even better—later on down the road.

It's more than "doing what you love" or "finding your passion." Those sayings get tossed around self-help circles like dad jokes at a family BBQ. But guess what? People's passions change. Some people never find their passion.

I'm not saying that you shouldn't pursue your dreams, you sure-as-shit should. But the universe has a twisted way of steering you in the right direction, and you gotta take those blinders off and be on the lookout at all times. Focusing too much on one dream can leave you imperceptive to the vast array of other opportunities that will be presented to you along your path. And they *will* be presented to you.

Success is always defined from your unique perspective, so the meaning is open to your interpretation. But to me it means freedom. Freedom to do what you want, when you want, and with the people you love. Freedom from punching a time clock. Freedom from the constant nagging worry of lack of money. Freedom of choice.

Success to me is living your life as fully as possible. And that's where the "passion" should come in.

You see, before I got into real estate, it was not my "passion." I didn't always want to be a real estate agent when I grew up. I wanted to be a professional baseball player. When I walked past a real estate office the skies didn't part, and I didn't hear angels singing or any of that crap. But once I got into the field, I threw myself into it with passion. Because if I do a job, I want to do it well. If I provide a service, I want to provide the best service I possibly can. And if I'm handed a golden opportunity, you bet your sweet ass I'm gonna take it.

But this book is not about real estate, or any other profession for that matter. It's about realizing that when you have an opportunity—you go for it, even if it's not the opportunity you thought you wanted. It's about being able to change directions when the road forks or ends at a cliff. It's about being open to every possibility that may come your way, and then pouring your passion into it. It's about acknowledging that when you fail, or don't get what you want, that's just the universe pushing you on to bigger and better things. It's about kicking ass and taking names in the face of adversity.

the paradox of failure

Did you make a mistake? Did something not turn out the way you planned? Good.

Maybe you needed to go through that to get where you're going next. Without having gone through it, you would never have had the opportunities that you have now or will have. It's something of a butterfly effect in that one seemingly insignificant event can dramatically change the outcome of an unrelated future event.

Know this: Whatever path you're on, whatever goal you have, it's not gonna turn out exactly like you planned. Plan for that. It might turn out *way, way* better.

Even if you fall flat on your ass at something, it's all good. Even if your lifelong ambition of becoming a pirate turns out to be nothing more than a puppet show wearing an eye-patch. You're better for it.

Trust that when things didn't work out, they didn't for a reason. The universe always has your back, and although you may not have known the reason at that time, you will. At a minimum, you'll learn a valuable lesson, see an insightful new perspective, be guided in the right direction, or get a sweet new ass tattoo.

There are, of course, some horrific events and situations in our lives that don't have a silver lining. I know—I've been scarred by my share of trauma, as you will read. What I am talking about here are those inevitable disappointments in life. Those times when your dreams came crashing down and you just wanted to give up. Those moments when you felt like the whole world was watching and judging you for being a loser. Those times in your life when you have failed.

But I say embrace failure. Love and appreciate failure. Respect failure. Failure is not the enemy but rather your best bro in a time of need. Your BFF when shit hits the fan.

I invite you to consider a new perspective: A perspective in which you consider all negative happenings as something positive down the road. Not just the mega life-changing events, but the mundane losses as well. The time you missed the damn bus and had to wait an extra hour sitting next to Crabby McCrabberson at the bus stop without your headphones. The time you bombed the interview for your dream job. The time you peed your pants at band camp, and everyone laughed at you. Yeah, the dumb shit.

Failure is a paradox in its most absolute form. Failure is a requirement of success.

The only way to avoid failure completely is to: 1. Lower your definition of success. 2. Never attempt anything in which failure is a remote possibility. Bo-ring.

Perception is reality, and the way you decide to interpret an event will dictate the reality you are about to experience next. This is law. You don't have to be some backpacking, granola snacking, tree-hugging hippy to benefit from this either. It's available to everyone. In fact, no one is immune to it. No one is above the law.

Whatever negative situation you find yourself in at this very moment is the result of the way you've been conditioned to think, the misguided beliefs that you hold so dear, and the subconscious feelings you have about yourself and the way the world works. But you can change all that right now.

To help you do this, I have added content to this book, including interviews with other entrepreneurs who have agreed to share their stories in hopes of encouraging you further on your own journey despite whatever obstacles come your way. You will also find sections for your own personal reflection (or what I call the "What About You?" — or "WAY"—pages). You may want to use a small notebook in which to write down your thoughts, so that you can look back on them at a later date. You might be surprised at how much you can learn from yourself!

Want to know more? Then turn the page to find out how I turned the epic shitshow of my life into the perfect shitstorm of success—and how you can too.

chapter one

make failure your bitch

"Whoever told you life was fair worked at a carnival."

— *Unknown*

Ever been fired? I have, three times in a row, in fact. Divorced? Me too. Lost your home? Been there, done that. Lost two businesses at the same time? That's me.

How about robbed at gunpoint? (Traumatizing, isn't it?) Accused of a serious crime, arrested, and prosecuted by the court of public opinion even though you were innocent and only *12 years old*? Yes, believe it or not, that really happened to me too.

I've been through a lot of shit and survived. That's how I know you can, too. Because I believe that with every loss you experience, be it your livelihood, your most significant relationship, your home, your sense of security, or even your reputation/identity, you will reap equal, or even greater gains. That's certainly what I've discovered over the years. The trick is to get through the negative feelings you have about yourself to see this truth.

But if you're like most people, you've been brought up to believe that suffering any of the above-mentioned losses makes you a *Loser*, as if you've been labeled with a giant letter "L" tattooed on your forehead. Society shames us for failing or for suffering any kind of defeat. And from a young age we are raised with messages like: "If you don't go to college, you're a loser," "If you don't make X amount of money or get married by a certain age you're a loser," "…loser…loser…loser…loser!"

And what happens to people as a result of all of this societal pressure? Ashamed that they are less than optimal human beings, they end up as liars. Just look at all the bullshitting that goes on in social media. Most people post all kinds of crap about how they're living their #bestlives because it appears they've reached a level of success and comfort where nothing bad ever happens to them anymore. Nobody posts their failures on Instagram, only the highlight reel of their lives, which, in turn, makes you feel sadly inadequate about yours.

No, I am not saying you should advertise all your failures on Facebook.

What I am saying is that you don't have to pretend that life is perfect. It's not. The path to success is a bumpy-ass ride down a slippery slope, and failures happen to the best of us. They happen to all of us. So, denying your failures and struggles is not going to help. Instead, facing up to your mistakes and learning from them will reap far greater benefits in the long run.

Yeah, it's going to be painful, and I'm sure you've heard the expression, "no pain, no gain." Well, as it turns out, I used to be a personal trainer as well as a competitive bodybuilder, and I can tell you it's the pain of ripping the muscles and repairing them into bigger, tougher muscles that makes us stronger and more resilient—and sometimes even champions. Without the temporary pain of reaching muscular failure, there is no growth. We all have the ability to turn failures into triumphs. To take what we've learned from them with us into the next venture. To turn disasters into dreams.

In other words, the bad things that happen to you, the struggles and the failures, are nothing to be ashamed of. They serve an important purpose: to help gear you toward the success you are meant to have. That's right, failures are the building blocks of success. You can make failure work for you. *Make failure your bitch.*

I didn't always know this to be true. But now I do. And I'm sharing this with you to help you turn your own defeats around and live a happier and more satisfying life.

humble beginnings

My own life did not start off promisingly. My biological father, James, was a piece of work, and when I say piece of work, I mean a real piece of shit. For instance, from birth until I was four years old, he used to constantly talk smack about my mom to me and my little brother. Like her own parents hadn't loved her, so we should just ignore her too. Like she was unworthy of our time and attention. Luckily, my mind was strong enough not to buy the BS he was selling. I had always known her unconditional love for me and loved her back. Him? Not so much.

James was an abusive husband and father. His abuse was mental, physical, emotional, and spiritual. He also abused drugs. Yeah, he was a real winner. So, I don't know if it was all the drugs he took, an undiagnosed mental illness, or a combination of the two that made him behave like a deranged monkey, but he did some pretty crazy shit in my early years.

First, he left my mom when she was seven months pregnant with me (his first child) after waking up one morning and announcing he'd dreamt that God had told him there was going to be a giant earthquake, California would fall into the ocean, and we needed to escape to Salt Lake City, Utah, ASAP. Since we lived in Livermore, which sits on the eastern edge of the San Francisco Bay Area, we were surely doomed. When my mother refused to budge, James packed up and left us in the dust (and alone to die a torturous death via the San Andreas Fault).

taking a risk

When he returned a year and a half later (apparently feeling that California was no longer in imminent danger), my mom took him back. Why? Mom says it was because it was 1970, and you just didn't have a kid without being married. Back then, it was still shocking and scandalous to be an unwed or divorced mother. And no one would employ single mothers either. "Who will look after your children? What if your child gets sick?" We're talking about a time in the not-too-distant past when it was uncommon for women to own a home or even a credit card. So, understandably, my mother didn't feel like she had much choice but to take James back. To outsiders, James appeared to be a kind of knight in shining armor.

But ultimately, she did make the decision to leave him and take us with her after enduring another year and a half of his crazy-ass antics. His movie montage of father-of-the-year highlights included: staying up for a week straight shooting methamphetamine so he could appear mentally unstable in front of the draft board (I don't think you needed help with that there, buddy); beating me with a hairbrush for walking between him and another adult while they were having a conversation, leaving me covered in bruises ("Don't cry and don't tell your mother!"); telling me and my younger brother that we'd be better off dead than living with our mother because she wasn't baptized Catholic (like he had been); and more.

That's right. He'd "found religion" before his return to California and thought he was holier than thou. In reality, he just abused the Bible like he abused everything else, making a show of reading it for *four hours straight* every night after coming home from work—instead of engaging with his family. He followed that with an hour of "drum practice" that consisted of his sitting behind a real drum kit and playing the "air drums" the whole time. He didn't even have real drumsticks. You've heard of marching to the beat of your own drum? This psycho marched to a beat only he could hear. Every day. For an hour.

At any rate, after a few years my mom got tired of his bullshit and did the healthiest thing she could for me, my younger brother, and herself. She decided that living as a divorced, single mother—even with all the side-eyes from neighbors and strangers—was better than remaining in a miserable marriage. I was three years old.

Reflecting on it now, it's clear to me that Mom was the person who first taught me to be a survivor. Mom taught me what unconditional love was, and she taught me an attitude toward failure that differed strongly from the opinion of the world back then and even today. There were many who viewed (and still view) a woman as a failure if she was divorced. "She can't keep a man," they'd say. "She must have done the marriage wrong." But it was James who had done wrong. He'd done us all wrong. He'd been the one who failed. My mother, on the other hand, had decided—public opinion be damned—it was better for herself and for her sons to be happy. After all, is staying in an irreparably damaged marriage really a sign of success? Or is putting it down, leaving it behind, and starting over with lessons learned closer to success's true meaning?

It's my belief that if you take risks like that, for the right reasons, they pay off. In Mom's case, the payoff came in the form of Gary, the man who, after she married him, became my stepdad, but who will forever be the man I consider my real dad.

what about you?

As I stated in the introduction, the "WAY" pages of this book are for your own personal reflection. Drawing from incidents in my life to use as a guide, I will ask you about times in your life when you may have found yourself in a similar situation or emotional state. And once you have the benefit of hindsight, I will then invite you to look more deeply into your own history so that you might see how the seeds to your future success may well be hidden—sometimes buried quite deeply—in the dirt of your past.

Now would be a good time to break out whatever notebook, journal, or computer program you use to take down notes. Do what works best for you.

Ready? Let's get rollin'!

I began life under the shadow of an unstable parent who created an unsettled homelife that lacked the benefits of emotional, physical, spiritual, and financial security. But while it may have been kind of shitty, it didn't stop me from becoming the man I am today.

Why? Because I let some of it go and used the rest.

What about you?

What kind of shitty stuff happened to you in the early years of your life? Did you have an abusive or absent parent? Or did you have emotionally stable caretakers?

What is your earliest memory of their attitudes towards money and/or success? Did they transfer any of those beliefs to you? Do you still share some—or all—of these same beliefs?

I understand that not all of this will be fun to look into. And I'm not saying that everything bad in your life is your

23

parents' fault, either. But being honest with yourself about how you began your life will help you better handle how you live the rest of it.

After writing down some of your memories, take some time to look over what you've written and pay attention.

Is there any past shit in your life that you are still holding on to?

Some of that shit needs to be released. Holding it in will constipate you—not just physically, but emotionally and spiritually, too. You can't move forward until you get rid of it. So consider this book to be a large glass of Metamucil and drink up.

My mother's risking the loss of financial security as well as social acceptance/approval when she left James resulted in her making all of us safer, our home life more peaceful, and her finding a much better husband and father for our family. I feel fortunate and blessed to have had such a strong and caring person at the helm during those formative years. Plus, Mom's actions planted a seed of resilience and hope within me that helped me to know that even if things seem really shitty, that doesn't mean they have to stay that way: I could change things. It was a good seed to have planted so early. I would need it to sprout very soon after, as you will see.

What shit—although bad when you first experienced it in the earliest years of your childhood—can you now at least appreciate as fertilizer? How can you use it to make you stronger? Wiser? Healthier?

In my case, as bad as it was for me to "lose" my biological father to divorce at such a young age, I learned early that you don't have to take shit from people just because they are blood. And don't let people try to convince you otherwise. The best person to look out for you is YOU. Just as they tell you on an airplane to secure your own oxygen mask before assisting others, you must take care of yourself before you can truly help another.

I also learned that people don't have to be related to you by blood in order for you to love them or be loved by them.

As you will see in the case of Gary.

chapter two

cat-5 supershitstorm

"We are all broken, that's how the light gets in."
—*Unknown*

Gary became the father I didn't know I needed.

He was an upstanding man in life and as a father. He was also in possession of both an admirable work ethic and his own business. He became the first real model of entrepreneurship that I got to see up close and in action. That would turn out to be a very good thing for me.

But first I would enjoy life as Gary's son. Although he did not recommend my going into the same line of work—"Concrete is back-breaking work, son, stay away from it."—he did encourage me to go into business for myself and learn to become more independent.

My mom is an amazing and loving mother, but she had very limiting beliefs about money that she herself had been taught from childhood. She couldn't help passing on this "lack mentality" to me and my brothers. She often used phrases like, "Money doesn't grow on trees" or "We can't afford that." Sound familiar? Luckily, I had Gary's living example: "You can start your own business and make your own money." He also employed basic human kindness principles to his business like treating—and *paying*—employees well.

I think I learned even more from Gary's example than by his words. Seeing him in action made a deep impression on me from an early age. As we grow up, we all receive messages about money and its power from our parents. Sometimes we are told things explicitly, like "Money is the root of all evil" or "Rich people are assholes." But we often learn from our parents' attitude toward money as well. They reiterate the beliefs that their parents taught them, and since we are born with no preconceived notions about money, we naturally pick up on whatever our parents accept as truth. It's a never-ending cycle, passed down from generation to generation.

For instance, when you were a child, were your parents hunted by debt collectors? Or were they always clipping coupons? Did they spend recklessly, or pinch their pennies? What sort of messages about money did you pick up in your childhood? What was—if you can recall—your earliest understanding of money?

The beliefs you acquired surrounding money in your formative years have more than likely stuck with you like a bad rash until this very day. But this, my friend, can be changed.

Gary taught me much by example—and not just in business matters. He showed me how to behave in the world beyond the office, too: how I should treat others with respect at all times because it's the right thing to do, and how being a good man means being responsible and kind.

When he married our mother, Gary immediately accepted me and my brother Matt as his own, even though he had a daughter from a previous relationship. He never made us feel less-than. He was as rock solid as the concrete he worked with.

Despite all this, by the time I was 10—and although they'd had a son of their own together, Jason—my parents sadly got a divorce. They loved each other; they just weren't *in love* with each other. Still, proving he couldn't be a more complete opposite of ass-hat James, Gary stood tall like a man, taking care of us, paying the mortgage and paying for our school clothes, and always making himself available to do father-son activities.

One of the ways he showed his love after the divorce was staying up till 4:00 a.m. on Christmas Eve each year so he could build the gifts from Santa while we slept. He would then show up again at our house at 5:00 a.m. to celebrate Christmas with us.

And there were those crack-of-dawn Sunday mornings when he would drive me around on my paper route. We'd load up his brown-and-orange Ford Bronco with bundles of thick-ass Sunday papers and wind our way through the neighborhood before daylight. Once all the papers were safely delivered to their respective porches (or an adjacent tree), Dad would then reward us with breakfast at Winchell's Donuts. That was the best. Well, Dad was the best.

Taking my cue from him, I still like to reward myself after a job well-done, only instead of donuts, it's usually something more like a nice glass of bourbon these days. Still, it doesn't quite match the feeling of satisfaction I had back in the day when I got to sink my teeth into those freshly made apple fritters: a well-deserved reward after an energized morning's work and the promise of a whole day still to come.

Do you reward yourself after completing a project or finishing a job—and doing it well? If you don't, I recommend that you start. The reward shouldn't be too big or occur too often. It should just be a small treat, and it shouldn't take too much time out of your day. (If the reward takes longer than the job you are rewarding yourself for, you're probably doing it wrong). A small reward is good for a little self-recognition. It's a fist bump you can give yourself.

Dad is no longer with me to enjoy those rewards. He's been gone for more than three decades now, but I am still as grateful today—or even more so—for all he did for me when I was growing up. If I have one regret in my life, it's that I didn't express my appreciation to him enough while he was still around. But I will give him the credit he is due here in writing, for all the help he gave me toward putting me on the road to becoming a better person. There was a measurable difference in the level of my confidence under the care of a competent father instead of a complete ass-wipe. For instance, at the time Mom left James, I was painfully shy, so timid in fact that my first day of kindergarten was an absolute disaster. The way Mom tells it, I basically hid under my desk crying until she came back to get me. Not a great start to my young school career.

Once Gary became my dad and things settled, everything changed. I must have been feeling much more secure because the turnaround was dramatic. I flourished. I got straight As. And I was good at sports—particularly at baseball and soccer. I was the only kid in the 9-to-10-year-old division in my hometown Little League to ever hit a home run over the fence off the pitcher (I wonder if that record still stands?). I even ended up traveling around the country—and Canada—with my soccer team to play in competitive tournaments. I never missed an all-star team in my childhood sports career.

I had reached the age of twelve—happy, healthy, and popular. Everything in my life was going great.

Until I was accused of being a rapist.

the shit hits the fan

It started off innocently enough.

I had a few friends—boys and girls—over to our house after school one day. Mom wasn't home from work yet, and we were hanging out, laughing, playing around—roughhousing, like 12-year-old kids do. We were being silly, acting like the stupid kids we were. Then, out of *left fucking field*, one of my friends exposed himself to everyone. There it was, his little 12-year-old prepubescent wiener, out for all the world to see.

This did not go over well. Everything stopped. "*Dude, what the hell is wrong with you?*" The rest of us guys were shocked, but the girls were—understandably—more so.

The next four days at school were as mundane as any other four-day stretch at middle school, USA. Math tests, lunch with friends, PE class, etc. But then, apparently, some girls started teasing the girls who'd been over at my place about how they'd been "partying" with a bunch of boys. I'm guessing that someone must have said something about the *wanker show*, because suddenly the girls were being accused of being "sluts" by the other girls. The girls started crying, and then, wanting to defend their reputations, they began spinning a story about how the boys had "attacked them." WTF? Where was this four days earlier?

The bullshit story spread like a raging forest fire, in gale force winds, in the middle of a 10-year drought. The icing on the proverbial cake was when the girls were called into the vice principal's office. Things were about to get *significantly worse*. The girls must have been sweating bullets under the hot lights of the interrogation room and not wanting to be caught in their lie or to be seen as harlots. So, under intense pressure from the vice principal to name names and report the incident to the police, that's exactly what they did.

Next thing I knew, little 12-year-old Chris, and the four other boys at the house that day, were being arrested and charged with sex crimes.

It was a shitstorm of the worst possible magnitude. A Cat-5 Supershitstorm. I was interrogated by the police, arrested, and criminally charged. I had my mugshot and fingerprints taken—the whole nine yards. At least I wasn't thrown into an actual jail cell. Instead, I was released to go home to slowly construct my own private prison of the mind.

The thing I remember most about this time was just how confused I was by it all. Even though I barely had an understanding of sex (let alone rape) at the time, I was now labeled a sexual predator in the local newspapers, seen as a rapist by all my neighbors, expelled from school, and was awaiting a criminal trial—all before the age of 13. I can't imagine the grief and torment my mother must have gone through, watching helplessly as her first born child endured the wrath of a system off its rails and out of control.

There I was, isolating at home, with no friends, no school, and nothing to do. I spent my days in front of the TV, watching every episode of *Gilligan's Island* and *The Price is Right*. I couldn't step outside my door without feeling the stares of my neighbors boring into my skull or hearing the hissing of their whispers behind my back. I felt very alone. I *was* very alone.

Outside of my family (my mother, father, and brothers had my back even though they were taking a lot of shit for being related to an accused sex criminal), there was only one other person who didn't turn his back on me. Mark.

He was my friend from school. He didn't do anything special. It was just that he stayed my friend. He came over, ate pizza, played video games, and we played baseball together.

Throughout the whole debacle he never changed who he was or how he treated me. I don't think I truly understood what a help he was to me at the time, though—how he was the only oasis in the desert. I was too busy going from sad to depressed to hopeless and finally to pissed off. I got sick of being a helpless victim of the system and wanted it to be over so that I could go back to living my life. Mark gave me the space to feel all these things without judgment.

I grew up a lot during that dark and difficult episode. I went from being an innocent kid who was happy with his simple life to a young man on a mission to clear his name. And as a result, I grew increasingly resentful of authority and establishment.

I started hating everything and everyone. I was angry and bitter most of the time and did not have an outlet. I started to question everything. The system I had been raised to trust had failed me.

But while this may not have been the way I would have chosen to grow into a stronger person, this is the hand I was dealt—and so I was forced to play it. The feelings I went through helped to shape my outlook on life. I'm glad that I let myself feel what I needed to feel at the time. I think that allowing children and young adults to feel how they need to feel is the healthiest thing for them, and that self-expression helps them to grow into the people they are meant to be. More on that in the next chapter.

So how did this situation get resolved? The charges were dropped.

The judge called everyone into his chambers before the trial started: the accused, the accusers and our families. Then he asked the girls' parents if —had they not been influenced by the vice principal—any of them felt the incident was one that truly needed to be tried as a criminal case in a court of law. The girls and their parents all agreed that it most certainly did not, and the case was officially dismissed.

Great! What a victory! Right? Wrong.

The damage—and it was severe—had already been done.

We tried to undo it as best we could. The families of the accused boys sued the school district and the police department, but after six years, we lost the civil lawsuits by jury counts of 7–5. Even more aggravating was that even though our names were technically cleared, the media didn't bother to report our innocence. It was old news. Boring. They'd moved on to the next thing.

My mother spent a great deal of money she didn't have on attorney fees to defend her innocent son. But even she says that the whole incident was a crash course in how to stand up for herself and what she believed in.

And this is what I meant about how the failures and struggles in your life pave the way for your joys and successes yet to come. You might not like how it feels when you are going through those things—you might even hate it, like I did—and it might take years to realize why something happened to you, or what benefit you got from it. But, trust me, during those dark and lonely times, you forge the tools you need to build your future success.

what about you?

I'm not a person who blames others for my failures, but I do like to give people credit where credit is due. That's another thing that Gary, my stepdad, taught me. He showed up at the time in my life when I most needed him, and he continued to "show up" many other times and in many other ways for me until the day he died.

So, what about you?

Was there ever someone in your life who gave you the support you needed when you needed it most? Even if they did it only once and you never saw them again, did anyone ever give you direction and guidance with no agenda other than to help you succeed?

Think back to your childhood. It might have been someone in your family, a teacher, a schoolmate, even a complete stranger. Whoever they were, they, when you were down, lifted you up and made you feel that maybe the universe was on your side.

Have you got someone in mind? Great!

Did you ever get to thank this person properly? Aloud or to their face?

I feel like I never truly expressed my gratitude—or at least enough gratitude—to my dad Gary for all he did for me. If the person you named above has also passed on, why not write them a thank-you letter, anyway? Put into words all that you'd have liked to tell them when they were still alive.

But, if they are still alive, then why not write them a real letter that you can send by post or email?

Or give them a call—or video call—or text them or try contacting them on social media, etc. I recommend writing a letter, if possible, because it gives them something physical to hold in their hands and refer to time and again whenever they wish. Also, many people find it easier to express in the written word what can be difficult to say face-to-face. Plus, since receiving personal letters through the mail is such a rarity these days, finding one in your mailbox can be a real treat. And when that letter is a litany of gratitude, it can be of particular sentimental value.

Certainly, the people who have provided more than their weight in gold in our lives deserve a little treasure to call their own.

Finally, is there someone in your life right now who *you* could be like a Gary (or a Mark) to? Someone who could use your friendship and support, your guidance or even mentorship? Someone you can help with no other agenda except to give them the boost that they might need?

If you want to be successful yourself, you have to help others on the road to success as well. And once you're successful, you'll need to keep helping others in order to retain your own success. No man or woman is a success without friends. And when that circle of friends is also successful, well, then you have it made. There's always room for another person to join the circle because it always remains a circle—it just grows bigger.

In fact, it was the importance of the support that a circle of new friends gave me that would be the next lesson I learned on my own road to success, as you will read about in the next chapter. It would also be one that entrepreneur Jennisse would learn, as she explained in an interview.

"i felt like my whole world crashed down on me"

An Interview with Jennisse:

Beauty Influencer, YouTuber, Owner of JayLee Beauty

Jennisse was raised by a single mother who worked hard to make ends meet. She dreamt of becoming a wealthy and successful businessperson when she grew up. I asked her to share her story and to share any words of advice that she thought might be helpful to you, no matter what stage of the journey you might be in right now.

CP: What was it like for you growing up?

J: I had very humble beginnings. I grew up watching my single mom struggling to pay bills and I always aspired to make something of myself to help her out. We never had enough money. There were times we didn't even have a car and it was really difficult for us to even buy clothing. So, I was always dreaming of having more—and of being more.

Dad left us when I was five, so my mother had no choice but to get a job and leave me in my grandmother's care. Some of my earliest memories are of me playing with my grandmother's things. I used to try on her ginormous heels and paint on crooked red lips with her lipstick.

I wanted to be like her. She used to make herself up so pretty. And when she did, I could see it lifted her spirits. Life was hard for all of us, but makeup had a way of making you look put together even when you were falling apart. Like it made you stronger.

So, my love of makeup began early! Like super-early. I loved it so much that I would do stuff like trade my new Barbie dolls for old makeup from Walmart. I was only five or something. But I was really happy with my trade. I definitely felt like I had really gotten the better part of the deal. I loved playing with makeup more than toys.

CP: Wow. So, when did makeup become a career for you instead of just a hobby?

J: It wasn't until after I had my baby. I had a C-section and was totally unprepared for how bad I would feel afterward. I was in a lot of pain. I couldn't even cough or sneeze without hurting myself.

I was really depressed about it, so a cousin of mine suggested that I watch something funny—like comedy videos on YouTube or something—to cheer myself up.

After watching comedy videos for a while, it occurred to me that there might be other kinds of videos on YouTube that could cheer me up, too. And I began looking up stuff like makeup tutorials.

After watching a bunch of them I couldn't help thinking, "Hey, I can do that!" Plus, I was lonely and bored and wanted to make friends. So, I decided to give it a try. I figured out the best time to film myself was when the baby went down for his nap, and that's what I began doing. I set my old camera up on a cardboard box and began shooting and posting my videos online.

They went viral instantly.

I thought I'd make like, one hundred friends, tops. But I got over a thousand hits really quickly. Some of my videos have now hit a half-million views. A few have literally had millions.

This got me noticed by YouTube, who asked me to partner with them. They were like, "We'll send you a laptop and equipment. You just keep filming out of your room!"

And I did well for a while until I began feeling...I don't know. Stuck. Like, I wanted to move on. Do more. I'm always like that. I want to see what's coming next. Keep moving.

When I was a kid, we didn't have a lot of money, like I said. So, I would go to my mother and say, "Give me five dollars and I'll turn it into twenty-five." And I would. I would use the money to buy bags of candy, and then sell the individual pieces from outside my bedroom window to passersby. My mom would then get her money back and ask for a loan on top of that! I was always business-minded, making deals, selling, and trading, trying to make a profit.

CP: So, you've been very entrepreneurial since you were a kid!

J: Oh, yes, definitely. So, when I wanted to be doing more, my husband reminded me how much I loved manicures and suggested that I go after my nail technician license. Nails and makeup are kind of related, you know, they are both about beauty, and this would sort of expand me as a brand. I began dreaming of having my own nail salon in a casino. So, I worked hard, graduated nail school, and in time was able to make that dream come true when I became the proud owner of a salon in a major hotel. It had my name on it and everything.

CP: You made your dream come true.

J: Yes! A nail technician license is pretty expensive, too! After a while, though, since I was working out of a casino, I began doing celebrity nails, which is where the real money is. This got me a reputation and then a second salon! I wanted to open a third, but then became overwhelmed with running the business. Managing a salon out of a casino is different from running your own little place on a street corner. There are expenses and fees and complications when you are attached to a name brand like that, and I couldn't keep up with the payments for it all. And I ended up losing both salons. Everything I worked so hard for. I had put all my savings into it, about $150,000 of my own money, and I still couldn't keep up. I was devastated.

CP: Tell me more about how losing your dream affected you emotionally.

J: I felt like my whole world crashed down on me, and I felt like a failure, like the worst person. It was probably one of the hardest times in my life. I even thought about suicide because I was so unhappy. Looking back, though, I'm kind of glad I went through that time because I believe everything happens for a reason. I'm actually really grateful that it happened because I feel so much happier now.

CP: How did you turn things around and pick yourself back up again?

J: I decided that I should have multiple streams of income. I didn't want to have all my money invested in just one business venture, because I saw that if I lost that one business, I lost everything!

So, I went back to makeup and began putting out more content on YouTube. I also kept doing celebrity nails, because I realized that I didn't need to have a glamorous casino salon to continue doing that. I could just work as a freelance manicurist.

My clients pay to have me flown to where they are because I know how to do their nails just the way they want them.

And I also opened an online boutique—we're talking clothes now. I run my beauty store and fashion clothing line through Facebook without having to worry about a store front. My brand is my own, not attached to anyone else's, and my sales have gone through the roof. I'm doing what I love, and I'm making other people happy.

CP: How do you make others happy?

J: People send me emails telling me how good and empowered they feel after learning makeup techniques from my videos. People love to feel beautiful! I love to make people up, too, and see how they brighten up when I've done their faces.

CP: What do you think you've learned from what happened to you?

J: I've learned that money isn't everything, believe it or not. That success is based on perception and that it's okay to fail because you can get yourself back up again. I'm so thankful that I wasn't able to continue with my nail salons. At the time they were what I thought my success was supposed to look like. But now I have something that I'm truly happy with. Plus, I get to appreciate family time in my current situation. I've grown a lot from those experiences because they made me who I am today and actually prepared me for what I had coming, which is what I'm doing now.

CP: Do you think you would have gotten what you have now had you not pursued the original dream of the beauty salons in the casino?

J: Absolutely not. I had to go through that first. Like I said, I wanted to commit suicide at one point, but I had my faith, and God really let me feel confident to move forward and keep going. I feel like that's what separates the people who eventually find success from those who don't: you've got to keep going. Don't be afraid of failure. Get yourself right back up again if you do. When I lost my nail salons and all my investments in them, I took a chance on investing another $50,000 into a business and I didn't even know if I was going to succeed. It was a risk that paid off and now I am selling out of everything!

CP: What advice would you give to somebody who is going through a similar experience where they were initially successful and then failed in a big way and had their dreams crushed?

J: That it's okay to feel like you're a failure. It's okay to feel like you're not worth it. It's okay to feel what you feel. Don't judge yourself for feeling how you feel: If you feel like you have to cry for a whole week, cry for a whole week. But then let it go. Because if you don't face it and you try to pretend everything's okay, it's only gonna get worse. It'll catch up to you, so allow yourself to feel that failure. Allow yourself to feel your emotions, process them. From my experience, I feel like my faith is what kept me going and I maintain that through prayer. And it helped me to get myself back up again. So, whatever it is that you believe in, use that to find the confidence to keep going.

Also, use anything and every tool you have to make yourself successful. I load up on key chains or scarves and give them out to people who've been kind enough to give me a shout out or a Yelp review because I appreciate that they've taken the time to do that for me. In fact, some of my business relationships have turned into friendships because we have supported and encouraged one another on social media. Being generous to others inspires others to be generous to you and helps make your own business grow.

I can genuinely say I feel so fulfilled in my life right now. God gave me everything I desired.

Jennisse's story is inspiring on many levels. She actually achieved her dream—but then had it snatched away from her. This brought her down to such a low point that she nearly gave up on life. But she did not let defeat win. Instead, she refused to give up. She held on to hope, to her faith, and to her determination. She found a new dream that she loves even more, and in chasing it didn't just pull herself out of the hole she'd been in, she took herself to the top of the mountain of success!

Her parting words of advice were to cultivate both an attitude of generosity—you have to give to receive—and a community of support among other professionals.

I, too, have found that having some form of a "tribe" is essential to success—as you will see in the following chapter.

chapter three

the oasis of anxiety

"Just when the caterpillar thought the world was ending, he turned into a butterfly."
—*Anonymous Proverb*

I had zero friends at my new school.

But since I had been expelled from my old one, and there were only two middle schools in my hometown of Livermore, California, there was nowhere else to go. Unfortunately, my "criminal" reputation preceded me there. I could feel everyone's eyes following me as I walked the halls, and I could tell they all thought I was some kind of perv.

I felt shut out and alone. As my bitterness, anger, and resentment grew, my feelings eventually exploded into a nuclear cloud of hatred. I was tempted to drop out of school. The only reason I didn't was because I needed the world to know that I was innocent, and dropping out of school would have been like surrendering to the system with a giant white flag. I was now a bona fide fighter.

I went into survival mode. I decided that if people didn't like me because I wasn't like them, then fuck 'em. I didn't want to be like them, anyway. In fact, I didn't want to be like anyone. I just wanted to be me, to live my life, to do my own thing, and do it my way.

That called for making some very tough decisions, like quitting team sports. Quitting baseball and soccer was hard because I was damn good at them. I even had dreams of turning pro. But after the incident, everything was different. My teammates didn't seem to look at me the way they used to. This change in atmosphere totally sucked the joy out of playing. After a while, quitting became a no-brainer. And that was it, I was done.

When I finally graduated middle school, I hoped to start fresh in my new high school, but that proved impossible. So even though years had passed, and even though the charges had been dropped, I was still seen as an ex-con or some kind of criminal. I may have been walking down new hallways, but I felt the same old stares and heard the same old whispers behind my back. I was a marked man.

And it wasn't just the students who were giving me shit. The teachers gave me attitude too. I could tell they didn't trust me. The thing was, I didn't trust them, either. Thanks to the living hell my former vice principal put me through, I had lost faith in the trustworthiness of adults in positions of power. So, we regarded one another with mutual suspicion. Predictably, my grades suffered. But I didn't really give a shit. Since I knew that teachers didn't have a clue about the real me, I wasn't going to let my grades define who I was to them, to me, or to anyone else.

oasis

That's when I began to find my tribe. They appeared like an oasis in the middle of the Death Valley desert that was high school: Other kids like me who also questioned authority, who not only didn't judge me based on what they knew of my past, but who actually accepted me just as I was, no questions asked. And I loved being part of that crew. We were the outsiders. The rebels. The punks.

Literally.

Because when I was 16, we started a punk band.

There were four of us and we had no idea how to play music, but we didn't let that stop us. We went out, bought some used equipment, set up in my mom's garage, and started playing. Raw punk rock music is not hard to play, so we learned quickly. We called ourselves "BHT" (because every punk band at the time had a three-letter name). I played guitar—all four chords, thank you very much—and we practiced nearly every day for years. We were so loud we could be heard half a mile away. Needless to say, our neighbors hated us, but we actually got pretty good—at least in our minds.

After a while, we started playing parties and live shows at bars and nightclubs in the Bay Area. We played the Gilman Street Project, which was an iconic punk venue in Berkeley, California. We even made a demo tape at a recording studio and sold cassette tapes at shows and via mail.

After our original singer quit, we reformed under a new name, "Anxiety"—fitting, right? I took over the lead vocals (if you can call it that), played guitar, and our sound shifted from punk to a punk/metal hybrid. We continued playing small venues and making and selling demos.

Our music was loud, angry, and aggressive, and our lyrics were defined by a general hatred of authority. They were often about fighting against both "the man" and "the machine," and there was usually a running theme that would elicit my now ever-present *question everything* mentality.

Here's a sampling from our song, *Greed Kills,* written in 1988.

Capitalist minds meet on the 20th story.
We're starving below, you don't seem to worry.
Get ahead of the next guy, the name of your game;
Power and profit, your story's all the same.
The foul stench of money fills the air as you laugh and joke about others' despair,
And you show off your fortune with material flaunts,
As you step on the middle class to get what you want.
Well, you make me sick with your monetary display.
In your world success comes to those who can pay,
So far, you've gotten by with your self-centered thrills,
but you'll be dead before you realize—greed kills...

Reading those lyrics now, you might think that my former self would be horrified at the idea of his future self-becoming a successful businessman. But I would disagree. I actually think he would be as proud of me as I am of him. Because the sentiments expressed in that song still hold as true for me today. I'll say it again: I may be pro-capitalism, but that doesn't make me pro-douchebag. I have never believed in exploiting others for profit or in crushing the little guy in order to make it. That sort of shit doesn't make you a big man. Just a giant asshole.

Being in the band was a cool time for me. We had the respect of the punk rock counterculture (at least in our hometown) and I was proud of us and the work we were doing.

We had dreams of making it big of course, although few punk bands actually do. I recall getting paid just enough after one particular show that each of us had the money to buy a soda, chips, and gas for the van. Still, it felt amazing that someone wanted to pay us actual money to play the music that we created.

I don't really know what happened at the end, but after about five years we decided to break up the band. Maybe some of us started getting real jobs or something crazy like that. Had we stuck with it, though, and continued playing and evolving our sound, I believe we could have made it. To this day we get emails from underground punk rock aficionados telling us how they have been listening to our music for years and still love it. And every once in a while, I'll pick up the phone and shoot the shit with a couple of my former band mates and we'll reminisce about the old days. But I don't regret moving on. Don't get me wrong, getting to make and perform my own music was just what I needed at the time. It was both a creative, cathartic outlet and a confidence-building early business venture. I look back on it with fondness and pride. But when I look back, I don't stay there. We can't undo the past; wallowing in all the "should haves" and "if onlys" is nothing more than a huge time suck. The only way to repair the past is to move forward with your life and make smarter choices in the future.

what about you?

So, what about you? What were your teen years like? How did your experiences then help shape you into the person you are today? The lessons we learned back then weren't always taught in a classroom. They could even sometimes come disguised as negative or unfortunate events.

In my case, although the whole experience was admittedly very traumatic, looking back on those years now I don't think I would change one thing about my time in middle school or high school—even if I could. (Well, maybe the part about my whole family having to suffer through them. My mom, dad, and brothers had to deal with a lot of backlash from being seen as the relatives of a "rapist.") The stress I endured from being falsely accused of a crime and having my reputation ruined before it had even fully formed was a lot to take for a kid of my age. It forever changed me.

But I think it changed me for the better. Looking back, I can appreciate how the experience strengthened my endurance, self-reliance, and perception—all qualities that would help me both to get past failures and to succeed later in my life. And who knows? Had I not gone through such a trying period of injustice, I might have turned out to be a big wuss instead! Or, at least, have ended up working for someone else my entire life, and never getting to experience the rewards of being my own boss and making it on my own.

There are two takeaways from this story that I recommend you reflect on. The first is:

Who is your tribe?

A real turning point for me when I was struggling and feeling all alone was finding my posse. Feeling accepted is important at any age, of course, and it's a major necessity in high school. However, no matter what stage in life you are in, finding a community to welcome (and not judge) you, is essential to your success. The members of your tribe are a rich resource for your personal and professional needs. In that pool you can find lifelong friends, work opportunities, financial assistance, and even future spouses. Even if you are more of an independent, lone ranger type, who likes to do things your way (cough, cough), you will find that you still need a community of some kind to help you succeed.

So where can you find your tribe? Communities, like clothes, come in all forms, sizes, and styles. Also like clothes, you will find that some fit better than others. Take a good look at the different groups of people in your life: childhood friends, classmates, co-workers, etc. Tribes can also be found in political parties, fandoms, competitive duck herding competitions, art clubs, rock bands, sports teams, you name it. And now, with the advantages of digital technology, you can belong to a tribe without having to share the same physical space.

If you don't already belong to a tribe, it would be a good idea to look for or even create one yourself. You will know that your tribe is your tribe because they accept you for who you are. That's the whole point and beauty of belonging to one. Authenticity is key.

Brainstorm a pool of different places, people, and ways from which you can find your tribe or extend the one you already have.

You can start by adding me to your tribe. Go to chrispatrick. net and let's connect. No judgment here, my friend.

And this leads me to the second takeaway from this chapter:

What is your outlet?

When I quit team sports, I left a tribe where I'd thought I would always be welcome, one that would afford me a lifetime membership. Until I found that my membership had been revoked.

Without that outlet to pour all the energy I had stockpiled from being healthy, young, and active—but also angry, frustrated, and restless—I had to find an alternative.

Luckily, I found something truly alternative: punk rock music. And the work of writing the songs, rehearsing and performing them, and even arranging the booking and travel for the gigs kept me quite busy. My mind and body were engaged, my creativity was stimulated, and I learned how to make deals and deliver on my word as promised. I'm still unpacking all the things I learned from being in a punk band. It was a gift that keeps on giving: part hobby, part passion, part business practice training. Having some kind of outlet is essential not just to enjoy success in business, but to being a success in life.

That's why the outlet doesn't have to be directly related to your business goals for it to help you to succeed in them. As in the case of Anne, a woman I know who made a pledge to herself to run at least two miles every day, first thing in the morning. She's kept that promise for three years running—literally. Without that outlet, she claims that she would be completely unable to adequately parent her four children, execute her job as a midwife, or continue her studies to become a registered nurse.

The outlet of your choosing, like your tribe, can come in many forms. Maybe you're someone who unwinds at the end of the day by knitting—especially after you discover that it not only is fun, but that it also relaxes the body, clears the mind, and often results in something beautiful and useful, like a hat, a blanket, or a sweater for your pet ferret.

Do you have an outlet? Do you need to find one? Below is a list of different creative hobbies and recreational and/or educational activities you might want to consider taking up that will enhance your life and provide an outlet for you in times of need. Circle the ones that sound the most interesting to you and then give one a try in the next week or so. Many online classes are available, so if anything below intrigues you, don't hesitate to investigate your options.

- Root for your local sports team
- Take a cooking class
- Learn a style of dance
- Start journaling
- Take a martial arts class
- Try your hand at writing a novel
- Write a how-to on something you have expertise in
  Learn to play an instrument
- Join a gym
  Start a band and make some music
- Try writing poetry
  Join a prayer/meditation group
- Buy a box of crayons and a coloring book
- Take a decluttering course
- Take an art class or just draw on your own
- Learn interior design

- Fake your own death
- Build a time machine

You never know where an outlet can lead. For instance, I found myself needing a new outlet for myself when Anxiety disbanded. Skateboarding neatly filled that hole for me because I was already doing it and there were no teams to join.

And skateboarding led to snowboarding...and snowboarding led to three big turning points in my life: a business, a funeral, and a wedding.

chapter four

zero fucks

"Great spirits have always encountered violent opposition from mediocre minds."
—*Albert Einstein*

What I liked best about skateboarding—aside from it being the athletic outlet that I needed— was that it was a sport with no rules. So, not only was it great for me physically and mentally, but there was also an outlaw status that came with it. It felt right and I loved it. I was all about doing what felt good to me, especially if it meant going against the grain.

Along with this lifestyle, of course, came the partying. I was never completely out of control, but I did experiment with all sorts of things. I never felt bad about that—and still don't—as I had always thought that the meaning of life is to have as much fun as possible. And that's what was fun to me at the time. I was all about rebelling against the norm and partying was just another way to do that. If I had a motto in those days, it would have been *Zero Fucks Given*.

I think that both a healthy dose of rebellion and a zero fucks attitude can be helpful on the path to success, so remember them, my friend.

As one might expect though, my grades began to go down the shitter. And truth be told, I barely graduated high school, squeaking by on the last day with a D- in history. I would rather have been locked in an overflowing outhouse at a month-long Grateful Dead festival than go to high school, but I *did* graduate. And I would want any child of mine to at least do the same. I've learned that high school is actually a great preparation tool for life because the adult world is overpopulated with fakes and phonies, and the sooner you learn to figure that out and how to navigate through them, the better. Hopefully, you'll have learned how to choose your friends based on their level of integrity rather than by their popularity.

movin' out

At 19, I decided that it was time to finally leave my hometown of Livermore. This place was holding me back, and in 1989, I moved to Santa Cruz — just in time for the Loma Prieta earthquake.

It was a massive earthquake and the damage it did to the Santa Cruz area in particular was pretty devastating. It forever changed the landscape—it looked more like a war zone than the peace-loving beach town it was. But it didn't scare me away. I decided to stick it out and make the best of it. I, for one, wanted to stay because it meant that I was finally free to be who I really was—without the judgments of others—and to truly make something of myself. Not that I knew how I was going to do that, but that didn't matter. The feeling of freedom trumped all. I believe that what you value most—in my case, freedom—will dictate how you live your life and what success will ultimately look like for you. Choose wisely.

The earthquake didn't keep me from partying, either. And to support this lifestyle I took a job with a landscaping company. I had worked for my Uncle Abe's landscape company for several years back in Livermore and learned a lot from him about the importance of a good work ethic—and the most efficient way to dig a hole. I rented a room from a couple of musicians who awarded it to me over several other applicants because I owned a guitar—thanks, Anxiety!—and I agreed to smoke pot with them at the initial roommate interview. I was still adamantly against doing things the traditional way—including periodically showering—and as a result, I grew dreadlocks and wore the same clothes for days at a time.

One day when I was skateboarding, I met Erick, and he changed the trajectory of my life with one simple question. "You want to go ride with us this weekend?"

Snowboarding, he told me, was a natural progression from skateboarding, and a hell of a lot more fun. He and his girlfriend went up to the mountains—Dodge Ridge or Big Bear—to board all the time.

Accepting this invitation, I did go up with him…and then went again…and again. Before I knew it, I was hooked.

Snowboarding was the greatest sport I had ever tried. For one, it was way faster than skateboarding and felt more badass. And since snow was (usually) more forgiving when you crashed (which was a lot), it meant you could take even bigger, crazier chances. It was perfect for a thrill-seeker like me, and I was immediately addicted. It also had an even stronger counterculture surrounding it than skateboarding. In 1990, it wasn't widely accepted or permitted at many ski resorts, and skiers and snowboarders often had heated exchanges on the mountain. I had found my calling. Soon, I wanted to ride every day, and nothing was going to stop me.

I was so obsessed that my visits to my mother (who had moved to Lake Tahoe by then) became more like visits to the mountains. It helped that my brother worked up at Heavenly—the ski resort right there on the lake—and could sneak me on for free wearing one of his Heavenly employee jackets. Like its name, that resort was truly a paradise for me. I was there practically all day, every day, and although I didn't see my mother much during the day, at least she always knew where to find me.

And one day she had to. I vividly remember riding the ski chair lift one afternoon and being shocked to find my name on the chalkboard at the top of the lift. The message read: "CHRISTOPHER PATRICK – CALL SKI PATROL ASAP." I did and they connected me with my mom. She had news that made my blood run cold: Dad was in a coma.

goodbye/hello

Shocked and devastated, my mom, my brothers, and I all piled into the car and headed back to Livermore where Dad lay in ICU on life support. He had had a brain aneurysm, his second. Day after day we would all gather around his bedside, hoping for improvement. Hoping for hope.

Since we no longer lived in Livermore, my Uncle Abe and Aunt Kay's bar became our home base. At the time, they owned and ran the Livermore Saloon, a bar that's at least 100 years old by now. If you assumed by its "Old Western" name that it had a bit of a cowboy vibe, you'd be right. Livermore was kind of *country* back then, and the bar was a staple in the area. With its solid wood bar, 20-foot ceilings, and olive-green walls—not to mention its stocked shelves—it was a comforting place to return to after visiting with Dad in the hospital day after day and finding his condition unchanged.

The saloon had been one of Dad's favorite hangouts as well. His go-to for Bailey's and coffee. Plus, it was a great place to blow off steam, get a drink, and play some pool. I know, because that's exactly what I did. And even though I lost every game I ever played against Uncle Abe over the years—he was an amazing pool player—I learned a hell of a lot. Getting your ass kicked, as it turns out, makes you better.

Another pastime at the saloon was karaoke, Uncle Abe's favorite hobby. My punk band past made me more of a screamer than a singer and I couldn't carry a tune if it had a handle on it, so I wasn't up for singing karaoke when I actually wanted to scream with Anxiety.

That is, until I saw Leilani.

You couldn't help but notice Leilani. She was a pretty, tall, and athletic-looking blonde with a great smile. But what really made me notice her was the Independent Trucks hoodie she was wearing. Yes, folks, it indeed pays to advertise. For those of you who don't know, Independent Trucks is a company that makes skateboard parts (the trucks being the metal pieces that hold the wheels onto the board).

Instantly drawn to her, I began chatting her up and found out a few things. Like, even though she looked barely old enough to drink legally she was actually a year older than me. Also, she was from Breckenridge, Colorado, which, from what she said, sounded really cool. It was a town in the middle of the Rocky Mountains with a local population of about 2,000 that was big into snowboarding (and skiing). Even though she loved that scene because she was all about boarding too, she'd ended up coming back to Livermore to visit with her dad and try to figure out what to do with her life.

We ended up playing pool and drinking together until closing time and then spent every day in each other's company after that. Meeting Leilani could not have come at a better time in my life. I was amazed and grateful to be able to experience the happiness and support of a first love at the same time that I was going through such sadness, anxiety, and grief.

It was a paradoxical time of both incredible joy and immense sorrow because after consulting with doctors and with one another, my family and I had to make the incredibly difficult decision to pull the plug and let Dad go. Turns out, the universe didn't feel that would be necessary, and Dad passed away that night on his own.

After Dad's funeral, we all went back to the bar to celebrate his life, remember the good times, and sing karaoke in his honor. To this day, we still pay Dad homage by having Bailey's and coffee at Christmas.

It was devastating. I was 21. I had never experienced the loss of a loved one that close to me before, and the shock of that loss caused a shift in my way of thinking and changed my perspective forever. After that, nothing ever seemed to be as big a deal as it used to. Numbed by Dad's death, I began operating from a new emotional baseline, never letting myself get too up or too down. In contrast to Dad's death, everything else seemed pale in comparison and didn't seem worthy of eliciting a strong response from me in either direction.

Except Leilani. She was the source of my happiness, the shining light in my tunnel of darkness, like the sun persevering through a rain shower.

I strongly believe that things—both good and bad—happen for a reason. That's why I don't reject the bad events that have happened in my past. I know they weren't enjoyable when I was experiencing them, and I'm sure many of you reading this would prefer that the difficult and traumatic experiences in your life never happened. I get it. However, I have found—and one of the main purposes of this book is to help you to see—that we should find ways to use what we learned from those times for our greatest benefit. Suck them dry for everything they've got. Turn the bad into good.

Meeting Leilani was the silver lining on the massive black cloud of my father's death. It wasn't like he left me Leilani in his will or anything like that (he did leave me something, as you'll read in the next chapter), but his exit and her entrance were connected as if by divine will. And I accept this connection as a gift from the universe that helped me to get through one of the worst times in my life and helped to point me in the direction I next needed to go to continue my journey.

And that direction was Lake Tahoe. Leilani and I moved there and moved in with Mom for the summer of 1991. I worked grounds maintenance for a hotel. Leilani took a job as a cigarette girl at a casino. We knew we wanted to snowboard full time and we had thought Lake Tahoe would be where we could do that. But, because the price of a season pass in Tahoe was very expensive compared to Breckenridge (where Leilani had connections), we packed my 1975 El Camino with all our worldly possessions (and our dog Indy) and headed to the Rockies.

Talk about independence and fresh starts. Leaving the state of California for the first time to begin a new life with Leilani was pivotal and exciting. Not that I had any idea what I would do for work or money, but I truly did not care. I had my snowboard, my El Camino, my dog Indy, and my first love with me, so everything would be all right.

what about you?

So, what exactly does it mean to give "zero fucks?"

It doesn't mean you shouldn't give a shit about other people. Or that it's okay to hurt them. Treating people like shit isn't badass or cool—it's just fucked up. On the other hand, treating other people right will always be right. So, let's not waste each other's time pretending otherwise.

What a "zero fucks" attitude *does* mean is that you don't give a shit about other people's *opinions* about what you feel, what you think, what you love. Do what you want. Life is too short to do anything else. You don't want to have any regrets on your deathbed, that much I do know. As long as you haven't been a dick to other people, and you did what you wanted to with your life and not what other people told you to do, you can die happy.

In fact, it is my belief that the closer you live to who you authentically are and give zero fucks about people telling you who you should date, or what music you should like, or what jobs you should take, the greater your chances are of not just succeeding, but succeeding beyond your wildest dreams.

Take the examples of the famous artists Henri Matisse and Pablo Picasso. Their paintings have become so famous that their names are practically synonymous with the word "artist." Because over time their works have become so commonplace, it can be hard to remember that back in their day they were rebellious to the point that at times they were rejected and reviled.

But even though they both had very different styles and opinions about art, they shared the same recipe for success: they gave zero fucks and did what they wanted to do.

They believed in themselves and their own abilities, and they were unapologetic about who they were. They did not let fear of public opinion censure or stop them. When the world mocked them, they continued painting. Wives left them, the media smeared them, and other artists sneered at them. Still, they painted on. And they kept it up until the world gave up and bowed before them, showering them with money and fame.

That's the way to give "zero fucks"—with style.

So, what about you?

What dream job or career path have you had that you haven't pursued due to fear and the discouragement of others?

What are some of the discouraging messages that you have received from other people? (Example: "You aren't smart/good enough." "That's stupid." "You can't." "That's not how we do things." "You'll never..." etc.)

Now go back and read those messages one at a time, but after each one, either aloud or in writing, answer back with something like, "I don't give a fuck."

Mean it.

chapter five

independence day

*"If you don't build your dreams, someone will hire you
to help build theirs."*

—*Tony Gaskins*

It didn't take long before Leilani and I sold the El Camino
for food money. But we didn't care. Nothing in the world
mattered to us except snowboarding and each other. There's
no greater feeling of freedom than the one you find at the
top of the Rocky Mountains on a bluebird powder day.

This lifestyle came at a price, though, so we both took jobs
at Breckenridge Ski Resort, which comes with a free season
pass, thank you very much. I was a night janitor, which left
my days open for snowboarding. And we hitchhiked back
and forth over the pass from Alma to Breck daily to work
and ride. We had nothing, but this was an awesome time as

I was completely free and was following my dream of living to snowboard.

After the hitchhiking got old, Leilani talked her grandfather into giving us a 1985 Chevy conversion van. There was one catch: we had to go to Iowa to get it. So, we took a God-awful *48-hour* Greyhound bus ride to do just that, and then drove it back to Breck.

It was worth the trip since we ended up spending part of the winter living in that van. We pirated our electricity via a 100-foot extension cord plugged into the back of a strip mall attached to a space heater in the van for warmth. The strip mall became our personal trailer park, and we ate burritos from the nearby gas station on the regular. The van smelled like dirty snowboard socks and fast food, but we had each other—and the mountain. We even celebrated Christmas in the van that year and "put up" a small fake tree my mom sent us. It was one of those plastic deals—maybe two feet tall at the most—green and plain. No lights and no decorations. But it didn't need them. The tree gave off just the right amount of Christmas spirit all on its own. I still have that tree in fact, and I display it every year as a reminder of those days.

For the next decade, I would snowboard one hundred days a year and make friends with lots of like-minded guys and gals who also squeezed every moment they could out of the day riding snowcaps. One of them was Mikey, a professional "extreme" snowboarder and one of the most beautiful souls you could ever hope to meet. With a permanent shit-eating grin on his face, and at twenty-three years old, he was already a nationally known athlete. We became very good friends.

I was living the lifestyle of my dreams: riding, drinking, partying, and shooting pool. As far as I was concerned, life couldn't be better, and I was perfectly happy with the way it was all playing out.

Leilani wasn't. Only I didn't know it. I thought life was great, and that Leilani and I were the perfect team. In her, I believed I had found my soul mate for life. Then I found out through the bro-network that she had cheated on me.

The shock of this news was especially severe because it was so completely unexpected. It was a blow second only to Dad's passing. I confronted her and told her to move out. She wanted to stay and make up, but I said hell-to-the-no. My refusal was part pride and part...well, okay, it was all pride. But I knew myself. I wouldn't be able to continue on with her, knowing what she'd done. I would have been incapable of putting it behind me or of ever fully trusting her again. She left town shortly thereafter, moving to Texas and out of my life forever.

The funny thing was, she had been the reason I moved to Breckenridge in the first place. She had introduced me to everyone. Now the town was more mine than hers and I was going to stay. The part she had played in my life had been important and impactful, but it was over, and it was time to make my next move.

And move I did: into an apartment with four or five other guys—some of whom I'm still friends with to this day, like "Mouse," who was not only "quiet as a," but a real stand-up guy who would do anything for his friends and a great snowboarder to boot. Life also moved on, and you know what? It was an amazing time. Life was still good because

I was doing what I wanted to do. I still hadn't been able to shake the smell of dirty snowboard socks and fast food, however.

One scene that took place in that apartment that I'll never forget was when Mikey came over to show me the prototype for a personalized pro-model snowboard that his sponsor had just released in his name. He was so excited that he jumped up and down on the couches and bed with a joy rarely seen. It was a monumental occasion for snowboard bums like ourselves and more than cause to celebrate. The very next day, he was dead. Killed in a three-hundred-foot- wide avalanche at Arapahoe Basin.

He'd triggered the slide while jumping a steep chute with another snowboarder—who survived—and was buried under three to four feet of snow for three hours before he was found—in his socks. The snowboard and boots had been ripped right off his feet in the descent.

That was a very sad time for our tight group of friends as Mikey was dearly loved by all. At the funeral, we all put little mementos in his casket. When my turn came, I slipped in a small bottle of Jim Beam since that was our drink together. It was very sad. Still, I couldn't help admiring how he'd lived: fully and for the moment, chasing his dreams to the very end. And how he'd died doing what he loved, which, I believe, is the most anyone can ask for.

His death also served to strengthen the relationships between our circle of friends. It was kind of like his last gift to us. So again, there was that sun shining in the rain.

what is freedom?

Mikey's death did not stop me from riding, however. Maybe I felt like I owed it to him to continue to enjoy something we all loved so much. Or maybe I felt it was better to risk death and live life passionately than it was to live a life with a safety net. Either way, I continued snowboarding during the day and working my ass off at night. (At this point, you might be wondering what part taking 10 years out of my life to snowboard plays in my success story. You shall see.) I took a job at a Mexican restaurant—ironically called Whiskey Creek—first as a dishwasher and later as a line cook. The place was eventually sold to new owners, and I was forced to look for other work.

Years later, this incident eventually helped me to come to the conclusion that sometimes when a door closes, it's meant to close. You just need to find another door that opens for you—and there will be countless doors to choose from. Sometimes you have to try a few knobs. If you listen hard, you'll hear opportunities knocking from behind many of them, and when you come across one of them, you just have to be brave enough to turn the handle and step through the doorway.

I didn't always think this way. When I heard I was going to be out of work, my first thought was, "I finally have a good job with people I like, and the business gets sold! Why can't I catch a break?" I had yet to understand how the universe worked.

But then opportunity knocked on a new door and I stepped inside. I was offered a job—as a manager no less— for a liquor store that I frequented. It was called...wait for it…"The Liquor Store." Because I'd been such a regular customer before getting the job, my roommates joked that hiring me to manage a liquor store was like *"trying to put out a fire with gasoline."* As we used to say, "you can't drink all day if you don't start early." Considering they drank as much as me—I literally had a running tab there that came right off my paycheck—I joked back that they should be grateful that I would now be coming home smelling like whiskey instead of tacos.

Despite the joking, I had begun thinking more seriously about things like job security, profit margins, and how to bring in more revenue. I just didn't realize it when it began happening. Although I'd found another job I liked, and was selling a product I greatly admired, I didn't want to be held captive by the decisions of others.

This new way of thinking had resulted from my reprioritizing what I wanted most out of life. Up until that point I wanted freedom, plain and simple—mainly the freedom to snowboard all day. So, I just took whatever job I could that had an evening or night shift and allowed me to do so. But it had begun to dawn on me that maybe I didn't really have the freedom I thought I had if it depended on my being employed by others in order to keep it. I needed *more* than freedom. I needed *independence*. And I had to figure out how to get it.

a businessman is born

Interestingly enough, it was at this crossroads in 1996 that I eventually received a $3,000 "inheritance" from the sale of my dad's business.

My dad's concrete company was not a big one, and after paying off all his debts after the sale of the company to the remaining partners, each of us kids ended up with a whopping three grand.

I suppose when most people say that they received an "inheritance" they aren't talking about an amount as small as $3,000. Still, it was a major windfall for me at the time. It arrived at the most opportune moment, too. And when I thought about how it was money earned with Dad's sweat equity, I wanted to be sure that I did something with it that would make him proud.

I noticed that the back storage room of the liquor store was not being used, and my wheels started turning. I figured I could make some sort of store out of it, but if so, it had to provide a product or service that Breckenridge either really needed or really wanted but didn't already have.

So, I thought about me and my buddies, our zero-fucks lifestyles, and those things that were unavailable in town that we were willing to go out of town to get. Then I had it: tattoos. Breckenridge had never had a tattoo shop! My good buddy Mouse loaned me another three grand to help buy equipment, and after locating and hiring a fellow snowboarder who had some experience with tattoos, I opened up shop. "Independent Arts" was born in the back storage room of The Liquor Store on six thousand dollars and a dream. It was 1996.

Although I had some limited business experience in the past, this was my first real business as a sole proprietor. I was very proud of the fact I had used the money from the sale of my dad's business to start it, too. I also learned that there was a thrill in the risk of starting a business venture that was not unlike the thrill I would get snowboarding.

Next, I hired another friend, only he had experience with body piercing, and we began to offer that along with the tattoos, as well as body jewelry and branded swag. After about six months, I was able to move the shop to an actual store front location on Main Street. Business was great. We're talking a gross income of over $100,000 in the first year. I couldn't believe it. With just $6,000 and a dream I had built a real, live, and successful business where none had existed before—literally created from the ground up. I felt very accomplished and proud.

When my body piercer had to leave town, I had him show me the ropes so that I could take over the position. And I asked that every piercing we offered be done TO ME. I thought that as the business owner, I needed to put myself in the customer's shoes in order to be sure we were providing the best service we could. I didn't keep any of these piercings long, but I do have a few holes (and tattoos) left as badges of honor. I also got pretty good at piercing others and had a lot of fun doing it. I ended up performing every body piercing on every customer in the shop for the next three years.

I could have lost my shit when my body piercer told me he was leaving. Instead, I took it upon myself to learn a new skill and provide the service myself. If I had known of any other body piercers in the area, I might have hired them. But since I didn't, I took the job upon myself. And I'm glad I did. It helped me to cultivate the philosophy that I still hold today: if you're going to hire someone to do a job for you, you should have knowledge of how to do it yourself.

This not only helps to keep you from getting fucked over if that employee leaves, it also makes you a better judge of your employee's abilities and a better and more understanding boss. And—maybe most important of all—employees respect a boss who knows their shit.

Know your shit.

Quitting The Liquor Store and opening up a tattoo shop was most certainly a leap of faith. Unfortunately, most people will never take a similar leap out of fear. Fear can be paralyzing.

At its core, fear is uncertainty of the unknown. The opposite of fear is, therefore, certainty. With that said, there are only two possible options: Stay where you are no matter how shitty and soul sucking it is. Or battle fear.

"The walls of your comfort zone are lovingly decorated with your lifelong collection of favorite excuses." —Jen Sincero

The reason most people never get out of their comfort zone is that it feels safe. Here there are no judgments. No surprises. No fear. And, conversely, no reward.

I was stuck in my comfort zone for many years, and I can tell you, it sucks. Much like donning your favorite pair of *give-up* sweatpants on your way to the grocery store, your comfort zone just feels easier.

Here, in this reassuring purgatory, there are no losses because bets are never placed. There are no losers because the game is never played. And there are no risks ever taken because it seems far too hazardous to give up the one thing that remains certain: your suffering.

The only thing worse than living in a never-ending loop of certainty is being forced to binge watch 72 consecutive hours of reality television. Unless of course you're into that sort of thing. The good shit is just on the other side of the walls of your comfort zone.

what about you?

Contrary to popular rhetoric, you don't need to convert your passion into your career. Sure, it works for some people, but sometimes putting a dollar sign in front of the thing you love just sucks the joy right out of it. On the other hand, your passion can be a springboard into the career you were really meant to have.

For instance, despite my passion for the sport, I never became a professional snowboarder, and Independent Arts wasn't even a snowboard shop. It did, however, cater to snowboarders and to people who lived the snowboarder/ski-bum lifestyle and aesthetic. People, in other words, who were like me. In fact, they were me. I was my own ideal customer.

Before answering the questions that follow, make sure you have a notebook or something similar to write your answers down. You will be brainstorming here!

Picture yourself as your own ideal customer. What is it that *you* love? What is your version of snowboarding— the thing you're most passionate about and build your life around? Write down whatever it is you most enjoy doing, the thing that makes life worth living. Is it an art form, a sport, listening to certain types of music, reading books by a favorite author, bingeing on a TV show, slip and slide tournaments, listening to podcasts, playing video games, or something completely different? You decide. As long as it's something that brings joy!

What are your top priorities? Having fun? Looking good? Getting healthy? Your children/spouse/grandchildren?

Reading comic books? Learning a trade? Finding employment? Write whatever is true for you!

The things you can't live without are: Your loved ones? Your faith? Your favorite sport? Music? Your favorite podcast? Your home routine? The sweater you knitted earlier for your pet ferret? Whatever they are, write them below!

What are the sorts of things you most like to buy for fun? What is the thing you will immediately throw down a wad of cash for the minute you see it—as in, "take my money!"—because you've got to have it even though it's not a necessity.

Finally, ask yourself if there is any product or service that doesn't presently exist that you wish did because it would satisfy a need or desire that you have?

You may have brainstormed your next successful business venture!

Take the case of Gela Nash. She loved clothes and looking good. Her priorities were the child she was having with her husband and staying stylish for the length of her pregnancy. The product she wanted but that didn't exist was a decent looking brand of jeans for pregnant women that looked as good as real designer jeans on non-pregnant women. (It was also the non-necessity that she would throw down cash for without a moment's hesitation.) Her very strong desire to continue looking on trend drove her to take matters into her own hands.

Gela began altering her husband's jeans for her own use and managed to make them look so convincingly store-bought that other pregnant women demanded to know where they could get a pair too. Orders started pouring in and Gela enlisted her best friend and co-worker, Pam Skaist-Levy, to help her scour thrift stores and alter as many pairs of jeans as they could to meet the demand. Soon a business *and* a baby were born—and both were named Travis. But when the clothing line branched out into T-shirts and tracksuits, it was re-branded as the multi-million dollar fashion line Juicy Couture. And it all started with Gela fulfilling the needs and desires of her ideal customer: herself. In addition to that, Gela was able to step outside her own comfort zone and face the fear of the unknown.

I also ended up expanding my business to include clothes. But the venture wouldn't end exactly as Gela's had. Instead, it all came to a crashing halt.

"it just blew up. it exploded."

An Interview with Rich Lopp:

Law of Attraction Teacher, Life Coach, YouTube Influencer, Tarot Card Reader

If you are like some people, you've never really had a "dream career." I didn't! You might not have even considered yourself to be particularly talented at anything. Never fear! This book is still for you.

Consider the story of Rich Lopp. Ten years ago, he started making YouTube videos that never really went anywhere, because, as he puts it, "I didn't really have a solid message to send. I didn't have anything that was worth anything." Predictably, his channels went nowhere, and he gave up on them. Looking back on that now, he'll also tell you it was a good thing he didn't find success with them.

CP: Why do you say that?

RL: I was a drug addict, and I was just young, stupid, wild, and crazy. And there's no way I would have been able to handle it. I wouldn't have been able to handle the money or the notoriety at that time.

CP: Weren't you drunk when you made the video that changed your life?

RL: Yeah. I made this video about the sign of Aquarius. I was so drunk I can barely remember making it, let alone uploading it to YouTube. Of course, I forgot all about it. Then, about a year and a half later, I'm surfing YouTube, and that video gets *recommended* to me—and I find out it's got over 20,000 views!

Then at around the same time, people started messaging me on Facebook asking for more content like that. So, I started making more videos about astrology.

CP: Kinda crazy!

RL: Right? What's crazier is that I'd get about 1,000 subscribers before I'd sort of run out of content ideas, so I'd end up taking a break from it again.

But one day when I'm bored, I begin reading tarot cards and filming it and loading it onto YouTube. The algorithm picks it up because I have so many subscribers and viewers for my other stuff. It starts recommending my new videos to them, and my channel suddenly takes off like wildfire.

It just blew up. It exploded, you know? My goal—I remember saying when I very first started reading tarot cards on YouTube, it was in September 2018—I said, my goal was by Thanksgiving to hopefully have 10,000 subscribers. I was like, man, I'm probably not gonna be able to do that. I'm a little stupid. Well, about Thanksgiving, I had 50,000 subscribers. It really took off and blew up almost immediately. And—from more of a universal perspective—it was perfect that way. You know, it worked out just perfectly.

CP: Well, that all sounds pretty accidental, or like "luck." What advice would you give to someone who has tried for years to achieve this kind of success without that luck?

RL: I tried making a successful YouTube channel for a decade before having any success. So, although it all sounds sort of "overnight," it wasn't. The biggest key to understanding success is that there is no such thing as failure.

> It's a learning experience, right? So basically, the only people who fail are the people who are stuck in the past and turn around and walk away and completely give up. There is really no such thing as failure: if you don't get what you want, if it's not successful right away, you learn something. I've reached a point in my life where I see everything that I didn't get as a good thing.

And once Rich's channel took off, he found that the care and upkeep of a popular channel like that was a full-time job. But it was one that he enjoyed doing and that he continues to do to this day, making sure to constantly put out quality content and to interact with and serve his customers daily.

It was much the same for me. I had never envisioned running my own tattoo and piercing shop. But once I found that I enjoyed it, had an actual knack for it, and could net a nice profit from it to boot, I worked at not only keeping it up, but expanding it.

That is, until I lost my main moneymaker.

chapter six

double down

"Only those who will risk going too far can possibly find out how far one can go."
—T. S. Eliot

So, how did a hard partying snowboard bum become a successful businessman?

By making partying and snowboarding a big part of his business, actually. That way, I was always having fun.

But it wasn't as simple as it sounds.

Independent Arts was doing great for a while and I rode that money train, sure that I'd continue to chug up the mountain of success for years to come. But new to the whole business thing, I didn't factor in the possibility of derailment. So, it came as quite a blow when I lost my one and only tattoo artist.

This sucked because tattooing was the shop's main attraction—what my brand had revolved around—and what provided my business with its most consistent source of income. I needed to find another tattoo artist—stat. But in a town of only 2,000 year-round residents, tattoo artists were hard to come by.

In the meantime, I modified the name of the shop to "Independent Arts – Exotic Piercing and Jewelry" and kept the place running. Since I continued to pull in a small profit and support my snowboarding lifestyle, I was still pretty happy to be a self-made man. I even had a new girlfriend (more on her later). But I wasn't quite satisfied. I had discovered what it felt like to have a booming business, and I not only wanted to experience that again, I wanted to reach even higher levels of success. But I didn't see how that was going to happen without a tattoo artist.

Then came Sierra.

enter sierra

I was a professional snowboarder—and a freelance tattoo artist. I wasn't in town long before, wherever I went, whenever people met me, they'd say, "Have you met Chris? You should meet Chris!" (Well, he went by the nickname "Gumby" back then.)

Gumby, Gumby, Gumby. That's all I heard.

Then, there he was, at the bar that had become my favorite hangout. I introduced myself, told him I was a tattoo artist and that I'd love to drop by his shop. He said, "Sure. Come on by." But the way he said it felt more like he was blowing me off than that he was really interested. Still, I went over the next day anyway and I really dug the place. I told Chris I'd love to work there, and he said, "Cool man, let's get started." And just like that, a business partnership was born.

We weren't business partners at first. In the beginning I just worked for Chris as an employee. And over time, I observed how he ran the place and grew to respect his work ethic. He amazed me, really, because we both snowboarded all day and partied all night. But every morning, there he was, vacuuming and mopping the floors of the shop, making sure the pictures on the wall were all hanging straight, and that all the jewelry in the front was neatly presented. He kept the place looking clean and professional at all times. It wasn't what you'd typically expect to see in a tattoo "parlor"—or what I expected from a partying snowboard bum.

> My respect for Chris grew all the more as he took me around town and introduced me to people (he seemed to know everyone). And wherever we went, people took care of us, giving us free food and drinks. It was like Chris was the mayor or something. He was definitely the most popular man in town. And I had the feeling we were going to get along just fine.

double down, llc

Sierra turned out to be so good that we could charge a lot more for tattoos. His presence and ability also brought an increase in foot traffic, and he quickly became an invaluable asset to the shop. Thanks to him, I was raking in the profits again and making more money than ever. So, it made sense to have him buy into the business and become partners with me. We split it 50/50 and called our LLC "Double Down Enterprises."

The term "double down" (for those of you who don't know) comes from gambling—blackjack, to be precise. It's when you double your bet in exchange for one more card. It's a risky move that can have a big payoff—an instant win. It also means to become more resolute or tenacious in taking a position or stand in something. The name was perfect for us because that's exactly what we would do when we saw the chance to double our business.

The snowboard store next door to the tattoo shop had moved to a different location leaving empty real estate just sitting there. It got me thinking, what if we opened another store there? And if we did, what kind of store could it be?

Sierra and I got a couple of notebooks, met in my apartment, and threw our asses in chairs and beers on the table as we brainstormed. We thought inside the box, outside the box, underneath, above, and all around the box. We listed the skills and experiences that we each possessed. We asked one another (and ourselves) what sort of stores we'd most like to see in the area. Again, what was missing? What was something Breckenridge hadn't yet seen? And maybe most important of all, what sort of hustle would we enjoy?

Since Sierra had experience working in retail, we decided that we would open a clothing store. But we didn't know exactly what sort of clothing we'd sell, until we had a vision.

what happens in vegas

For years I'd had a fascination with the whole idea of Las Vegas culture and its party vibe. The drinking, the gambling, the hot women, the loads of cash…it all seemed an ideal way to live. And since the idea of even opening another store was quite a gamble anyway, we figured, why not make Vegas the theme of the store? Especially when all the other stores just sold ski and outdoor apparel. We'd stand out, I figured. Big time.

We called the store "Jimmy Vegas – High Rollin' Fashion" and went the whole nine yards with the Vegas theme. Even though what we really sold was flashy street and club wear, we set up the store like a little casino. Display tables were made to look like roulette, blackjack, and craps tables and customers were even given "chips" with their purchases to "gamble" as store credit in the future. And believe it or not, we trained our cashiers in blackjack and even taught them to—you guessed it—double down.

We thought big. For instance, Sierra spent hours (200 by his own estimation) painting a huge mural of the Las Vegas skyline on the back wall of the store. And then, when we finally opened, we threw a bash for the ages. It was more like a town party than the grand opening of a store. But it worked really well, and we sold a lot of stuff.

We did so well, in fact, that we had to pick up two more tattoo artists. We sold merch at the clothing store, too. We had it rigged so that the buzzer for each shop could be heard at either location. That way, if an employee was in one shop but heard someone buzzing the door of the other, they could easily go over and take care of the customer. Sometimes a customer had to browse one shop before being seen at the one they intended to go to, but they never minded, because, in the end, they were basically the same clientele and usually did their shopping at both places anyway.

After a while though, the locals in town had all bought what they wanted from the store and the tourist trade—which lasted only about half of the year—couldn't really pull in the numbers we wanted. Sierra and I then found ourselves needing to move products and having to figure out how to do it.

the jimmy vegas school of marketing

We started buying themed merch and throwing parties to go with them. We had an Exotica Ball one month, an S&M Ball the next, and a full-blown rave the next. We'd sell tickets to the events as well as stocking and selling the most appropriate outfits that people could (or should) wear to each event. We created reasons for people to come in to buy merch and it worked.

I also started throwing "Casino Nights" at my place. (I was nothing if not always on brand.) I'd have 10–20 people over. Friends of mine helped out: some as dealers, one as a doorman, and another even worked as a cocktail waitress. It was hilarious. We served free drinks and they played all night. Our mantra was "Keep them drinking, we'll get the money back," and we did. In the end, the house always wins. The house take was a nice little bonus, but the times we had at "Gumby's Casino" will live on in infamy.

Plus, our shit was legit as hell. We used to get all our casino equipment and paraphernalia—as well as all of the clothes for the store—from the real Las Vegas itself. Sierra and I would fly to the fashion trade shows twice a year and choose the flashiest stuff we could find. It was all stuff that we thought looked cool. But since we were new to the business, we made some mistakes.

"The things that go wrong often make the best memories."
—Gretchen Rubin

First of all, Breckenridge is a ski town—that means a town of sweaters, coats, hats, and sportswear. Meanwhile, we were buying halter tops and booty shorts—things we'd like to see the women wearing to show off their assets, not thinking how they'd actually all be freezing their assets off. It was only after some women complained to us about it that we even realized there might be a problem. Then there was the fact that we were buying the clothes in super small sizes (like 2 and 3). As one woman asked us once, "Don't you have any clothes for normal-sized people? All you have are stripper sizes."

Other mistakes we made include the mural that Sierra painted. Oh, not the actual art itself. He did a great job. The idea was a good one, and I think it really worked. But looking back, it's obvious now that it would have been smarter to have hired someone else to do it or to have posters printed and hung on the wall or to have found some other alternative to Sierra's taking so many hours to finish it when his time could have been put to better use, working with me on planning our grand opening.

And the biggest mistake of all was the one we made in our first year: we didn't write off our trips to Las Vegas as business expenses on our tax returns. Talk about a fuck up! Yes, we indulged in drinking, partying, and gambling on those trips as well as doing business, but so did every other professional clothing merchant who went to those Las Vegas trade shows. That was basically the point of having those events hosted in Las Vegas in the first place. And Sierra and I always came back from those trips with inventory for our store (and massive hangovers), so they were legit business expenses. Just…very enjoyable ones. And again, very much on brand.

But we didn't realize this mistake until tax time when it came to bite us on the ass. We had proudly completed our first year of business and, while we didn't have as sizable a profit as we wanted, we were proud of ourselves. That is, until we had to pay out a big chunk of those profits to the government in taxes. We didn't make the same mistake (or hire the same accountant) the next year. A professional accountant showed us the ropes the second time around and really helped us to understand how it all worked. He even helped us to recoup most of our money from the previous year.

It was a learning curve, but we learned a lot.

ridin' high

I had become a big fish in a very small pond. I had a ton of friends and the respect of everyone as one of the few business owners in town. I reveled in being an alpha dog and was always looking for ways to spread that joy around so that others—not to mention my bank account—could benefit from it as well. One way I did this was by throwing barbeques on the street between the two shops. They were pretty epic if I do say so myself. There was tons of food on hand and drinks were free-flowing (all provided by the shops). There was even a kiddie pool! The events paid for themselves (well, the tattoos paid for them) because we always did great business on barbeque days, and they helped create brand awareness.

Another way we combined generating business with building up the community was with the Jimmy Vegas High Rollin' Bowling League. You read that right. We started a bowling league and had custom-made bowling shirts that came in a number of styles, all of which we sold at the shop. They could even be personalized—custom embroidered with the name of your choice. (We sold 64 of them! A pretty big "league" in such a small town.) And we made the most of them by shutting down the bowling alley on Sunday nights so that the "league" could get together and have big-ass bowling parties. Every one of the events we ever had, be they balls, casino nights, barbeques, or bowling nights, sold out.

I was ridin' high on life, so I guess it was inevitable that I would come in for a crash landing.

It was a warm spring day in 1999. The only resort open this late in May is Arapahoe Basin—the extreme skiers' and riders' playground. With an elevation of over 13,000 feet, A-Basin as it's called, is known for its steep terrain and long seasons. And now, unfortunately, it was the last place our beloved Mikey was seen alive. I was out tearing it up with a few friends as usual when we all decided to take the giant kicker directly under the main chair lift. It was very much a "Hollywood" jump. Which means, of course, that you go as big as possible to show off to those watching from above. The partly cloudy sky created what we call "flat light" conditions on the snow, so visibility was not ideal for big air (or for you if you plan on seeing farther than your arm). I carried a little more speed into the jump than I had planned and went big. I don't know how big to be exact, but it felt huge, and I was hauling ass. I stuck the landing in wet slush and found myself doing 35+ MPH directly against the grain of the deep ruts of an incoming traverse—like driving your car across the tops of 1,000 consecutive speed bumps at 100 MPH—blindfolded. I couldn't stop. I couldn't turn. And I couldn't see. I could only watch helplessly for the final three seconds as the giant steel lift tower loomed before me, growing larger and larger, closer and closer. I braced for impact.

what about you?

Are you an entrepreneur who currently has a business that's doing "okay" but would like to see it doing great instead? What are the ways that *you* can "double down" to make this happen?

I suggest taking out your notebook, going over the chapter you just read, and using it as a guide or checklist of ways you can help to make your business explode as mine did.

Let me take you through it:

1. I hired (an) excellent employee(s). "You have to spend money to make money." It's an old adage for a reason. So is: "You get what you pay for." If you want your business to not just do well but go big, hire good people and pay them well. This is not the place to be cheap or cut corners. A lot of problems can be avoided or corrected if you have the right, intelligent, and capable people in place.

> **In a nutshell:** Consider hiring quality help. Write down the pros and cons to having employees (depending on how ready you are to increase in size) as well as the possibility of replacing employees you might already have if they are not the asset to your business that they should be. Be sure to hire the best quality staff you can find and pay them what they are worth.

2. Consider a partnership. Is there someone you can partner with? Is there someone who shares your vision and who is willing to put in the hard work of growing a business? Some of the biggest businesses

started off as business partnerships. The list is long: William Procter and James Gamble, Wells Fargo (Henry Wells and William G. Fargo), Hewlett Packard (Bill Hewlett and Dave Packard), Ben & Jerry's (Ben Cohen and Jerry Greenfield), Birchbox (Katia Beauchamp and Hayley Barna), SoulCycle (Elizabeth Cutler and Julie Rice), OWN network (Oprah Winfrey and Gayle King), Apple Inc. (Steve Jobs and Steve Wozniak). Not to mention Microsoft, Google, Intel, etc., the list literally goes on and on. And let's not forget that Mark Zuckerburg would have been nowhere without Sheryl Sandberg's taking Facebook to the stratosphere.

I personally have found the partnership model to be the most lucrative and rewarding for me.

It may not be for you, but I invite you to give it some serious consideration. Make a list of potential people you can reach out to who you feel have the experience, interest, and ability to build a company—or perhaps even an empire—with.

3. Make sure that the business you build fills a need or offers something new. **Can you write a tagline or description of your business in one sentence that explains who you are and what you offer?** For me, our brand name said it all, "Jimmy Vegas – High Rollin' Fashion."

In our case, there were no tattoo parlors in Breckenridge, yet both the residents and tourists in the area were of the "snowbum" culture, a culture that is very tattoo-friendly. By providing a service/product that was in-demand and having the work itself done by a skilled artist, our shop was always busy. By selling complementary products—jewelry for piercings and "cool" clothes—that were also unavailable anywhere else in the area (remember all the other stores sold skis and sweaters and coats, etc.) our two stores supported one another. We ended up carving out a big presence in a small town—and even enhanced its identity through our brand.

> **In a nutshell:** finding out what makes you unique helps you to define your brand and increases your chances of success.

4. Can you create events that will help publicize your brand or product(s)? Sierra and I threw theme parties in town and created a demand for products we already had. We always did great sales as a result.

With today's internet, it can be even easier if you play your cards right. Musicians hold Zoom concerts. Galleries run art competitions. Just as they had to brainstorm money making alternatives, you can, too. JayLee Beauty sells her products live online on Facebook, like a mini QVC. She lets her followers and customers know when she will next be having a sale and invites them to tune in like an "event." There are many ways to grow patronage by extending yourself and thinking about how you can enhance the quality of your customers' lives.

Use this time to brainstorm ways you can do this yourself. The ideas you come up with that excite you the most are the ones you should follow through with!

5. **Finally, consult professional advisors.** If you know a good lawyer, accountant, or tax pro, use their services when it's important—especially in a legal sense—to do so. They will save you time, money, and pain in the long run. It's best to ask around before you are desperately in need of help: **Collect the names and contact information of reliable consultants from friends or business contacts that you respect, so that you have them when you need them.**

"my big dream was to have a child and start a family."

An Interview with Erin, Part 1
Mom, Wife, Business Owner, Coach, Activist
for Women's Empowerment

Sometimes the only way to get what you want is to go after it at full throttle. Erin knew this. It was the way she had always lived her life. It had obviously worked, too, because when we find her in this story, she's living a nearly picture-perfect life: she's got a happy marriage, a successful career—even a million-dollar mansion. The only thing missing from the picture inside the frame is the thing she wanted most in the world: a baby.

So, she did what any intelligent, self-respecting, go-getter would do: she made it the next goal she wanted to cross off her list and made sure she did all she possibly could to make it happen. Only things didn't quite go as planned.

CP: Hello, Erin. Please share with our readers your dream of having a baby and what you did to make your dream into a reality.

E: Yes. So, my big dream was to have a child and build my family. When my husband and I got married in 2018, we wanted to start our family pretty much right off the bat. As having children of our own was not in the cards for us, we started seeking out fertility treatments. But when we realized that wasn't the way for us to go either, we decided to look into adoption.

In early 2020, we located an adoption facilitator, signed the contract, and started the process of building our family through domestic infant adoption. It was a lot of work, but we did it all: home study, background checks, fingerprints, everything! It was a lot, a lot, a lot of paperwork. But we knew it would all be worth it since they were using all of that information to build our profile to send out to expectant mothers who were looking to choose a family for their unborn child.

CP: Sounds like you did everything right. So, what happened next?

E: We received our profile book back from the company, and I instantly put it online and on social media, because you never really know with adoption where your child can come from.

A few days later, we received a direct message on Instagram from an expectant father, letting me know that they found us on Instagram, and that they liked our profile and they wanted to meet us.

CP: That quickly?

E: Yes! It sounds almost too good to be true, doesn't it? Maybe there's a reason for that.

We sent messages back and forth for a while, but nothing really happened to move the adoption forward. At around the same time, my husband and I continued working with the agency and getting our home study done. About a month later, I got a direct message from the expectant mother. It definitely caught me off guard. But when we started talking on the phone, we each liked what we heard from the other, and soon afterward we met with her and her husband—and the infant son they already had—at a park by her home.

That meeting went really, really well. My husband and I felt pretty good about it. We just knew we would be officially matched with the family—and we were! This was back in August of 2020.

Things began moving forward. We were getting agencies involved and social workers and began extending financial support to the expectant mother as well. Then the woman and I began building a relationship. I went to all of the doctors' appointments with her, too. It was amazing. We really bonded. I felt almost as though I was going through the pregnancy with her.

CP: Sounds great. So, what went wrong?

E: Even though everything was going really, really well, there started to be a few red flags with some of the things that she was saying to us. But my husband and I just kind of brushed them aside because this was our first experience with adoption, and we were just so excited.

In October, I read on one of the woman's social media pages that she was starting a YouTube channel to document her pregnancy. I thought that was very, very strange, especially since there was no mention of adoption or anything. I reached out to our social worker about it, and she said, "Okay, be wary."

CP: So even the social worker thought things sounded fishy?

E: Yes. She warned me. And since I was still feeling that something wasn't right, I visited the expectant mother's Facebook page and saw that she was sharing all of the ultrasound photos—including those 3D/4D ones that we took her to and paid for out of pocket. I knew at that moment that she did not intend to place the child with us.

I called the social worker, told her what I'd discovered, and said, "I don't know if she's had a change of heart or if she's been scamming us all along, but we can't go forward with this match." That was back in October, about two days before my 35th birthday, so I was absolutely wrecked.

CP: Can you elaborate on some more of the emotions you felt at the time of the failed match?

E: Oh God, it was awful. I don't wish that feeling on anybody. It actually felt like a death. I knew that in adoption there are a lot of things that can happen: failed matches, failed placements, changes of heart. And of course, I would never fault anybody for wanting to parent their child. But how it all went down was just really gut wrenching for me. Like someone had punched me in the stomach. Especially when I first saw that post! It was a feeling of absolute betrayal because I had gotten to know the woman on a very personal level and had considered her a friend. I mean, I loved her so much for what she was doing for our family, so when it all fell through, it led into a downward spiral of depression that I tried to hide from my husband and mother-in-law. I mean, for the first couple of days, I couldn't even get out of bed. And then, when I did manage to force myself to get up in the mornings, I would sit at the computer and stare at the screen, unable to work. I just felt so lost and empty. Like I was broken, and no one could fix it. It was awful.

This lasted for about six weeks.

CP: How did you manage to get out of that deep funk?

E: Well, it basically took a "come to Jesus" moment from my husband. And this is where the universe works in amazing, beautiful, and mysterious ways.

My husband had basically seen enough—not that he wasn't feeling for me and didn't want to help me—that couldn't be further from the truth—but he finally had to say some things that were extremely uncomfortable to hear. And I needed to hear them, because the depression from this failed match was really taking a toll on our marriage.

I didn't want to let this woman dictate my happiness, or how I feel for what I don't have, and I really wanted to focus on what I do have. And once I realized that it was affecting my husband in such a way that he was feeling disconnected, I snapped out of it.

It was like I hit a wall and I said: You know what? Come tomorrow, I'm not letting this girl hold my emotions anymore. It happened. I don't know why it happened, but maybe it's a learning lesson, and we're moving on. We're moving forward. I'm gonna be positive. I'm gonna look toward the future, and whatever is going to happen is meant to happen. And it's all in God's plan.

CP: How were you able to move on?

E: My husband sat me down and we had a heart-to-heart about not giving up and looking forward in hope. He believed that we would get the child that was meant for us and asked me to believe it, too. I promised him I would push forward and think more positively about not just making another match, but the match that was right for us.

Then, *the very next day*, the phone rang.

(To be continued…)

As I said at the beginning of this interview, oftentimes going full throttle will get you to your goal. Other times, it can mean you are going so fast that you miss what's flashing past you.

Like those little red flags that started flapping around Erin the more she spent time with the expectant mother of the child she hoped to adopt. Erin didn't actually miss the flags as much as she refused to look too carefully at them for fear that they would tell her that the adoption process was going to fall through. But her gut knew the truth. Her heart and mind just weren't ready to accept the message it was sending them.

Where we last left *my* story, I, too, had been getting messages from my gut. Messages like, "It's time to move away and move on." But I wasn't listening to them either. Instead, I was barreling down the mountain at top speed, unable to stop myself from the unavoidable collision with a steel lift tower and almost certain instant death.

chapter seven

taking inventory

"Everything happens for a reason, and sometimes that reason is that you're an idiot."

—Chris Patrick

"Take inventory!"

A man on the chairlift yelled down as I coasted backward to the bottom of the mountain—my snowboard broken in two.

Dazed and confused, and in a world of hurt, I was met there by Ski Patrol, who'd obviously been alerted to the crash. "You know where you are?" "You know your name?" "You know what day it is?" Typical concussion protocol when someone hits an inanimate object at warp speed. Thank God I didn't hit my head. One second before impact I had thrown my board up at the lift tower in hopes that my legs could absorb the hit. They didn't. My back did. So, while I had saved myself from certain death with the last-ditch effort, my back was so fucked that I could barely walk.

I couldn't even bend my legs enough to get into a car and had no choice but to take a miserable thirty-minute ride back home in the bed of Mouse's Toyota pickup truck. As I lay there staring up at the now bluebird sky, the beat up '85 Tacoma limping back to safety, I knew my snowboarding days were over.

Danielle, my girlfriend at the time, was helpful in taking care of me afterward. But I was laid up on the couch for three months straight watching TV. It reminded me of those months when I was awaiting trial and was stuck at home watching a mind-numbing amount of Gilligan's Island.

Once again, I felt isolated, alone, and unable to do much about my situation other than to wait it out and feel pissed off. Only this time, I was numbing the pain with black market muscle relaxers and a bottle of Absolut Citron a day. It was awful. My back injury plagued me for many years after that, too, and each time it flared up, it felt like a sword was being shoved all the way through me. Like being impaled by King Leonidas of Sparta.

I dealt with my injury on my own terms, though, and didn't go to the hospital until months later. I was told I had broken my ribs and that there wasn't anything they could do to speed up the healing process anyway.

I did, however, use the time that I was down to take inventory of my situation and I found a lot to be grateful for. I was in pain, but I could walk, I was not paralyzed. My head was in one piece, and I could still think. I had both an awesome girlfriend and a great roommate (Mouse) to look after me. Finally, I even had a business partner who could mind the stores and oversee our employees while I was away.

Still, with my back in constant pain—even once I had recovered—snowboarding became a lot less enjoyable. The discomfort and limited mobility put a damper on my whole experience with the sport I had loved for nearly 10 years. The carefree and reckless style that is necessary to fully enjoy snowboarding had been taken away. And things only got worse the following year when I broke my ankle while drunken house-wrestling with a friend and had to take the next six months off from riding altogether.

I have said before that everything happens for a reason, and sometimes that reason is that you're an idiot.

But seriously, my idiocy worked to my advantage, because it was time for a new chapter in my life to begin. And without those accidents putting an end to my snowboarding years, I might still be there now, riding my life away, never growing beyond the tiny snow globe of Breckenridge. As I've expressed before, I don't think it's worth beating yourself up over the failures or fuck-ups in your life. Instead, I believe they should be examined and seen for what they truly are: signs from the universe telling you it's time for something new.

changes

Around this time, I had also started seeing a new girl: Mackenzie.

Danielle and I had drifted apart, as couples do, a while earlier. Mackenzie was a massage therapist who worked upstairs from one of my shops. A mutual friend of ours had suggested that we get together because he knew that we both liked to knock one (or two…or three…) back. So, I invited her to go out to the bar one night and we proceeded to get completely shit-faced. We made this a regular occurrence and next thing you know, we were dating. I loved her sarcastic sense of humor, dry wit, and passion for martinis. I began seeing her as someone I could share my future (and drinking habit) with.

And my future was beginning to take shape. Because I could no longer enjoy snowboarding as I once did, I began to seriously think about moving. What was the point of staying somewhere where it was cold all of the time if I couldn't take advantage of the snow? There was only one place I could think to move to though, and it certainly wasn't cold there: Vegas.

The decision did not come easy. I had lived in Breckenridge for the past decade and built my businesses from the ground up. Still, I'd been mentally checked out for a while—"taking inventory" ever since the first accident. I knew it meant going from being a big fish in a small pond to a guppy in the big-ass ocean, but it had to be done. Yeah, it was scary, but I liked to take risks, and Las Vegas seemed to be the best place to take a gamble.

But that didn't mean I was closing up shop or abandoning Breckenridge. On the contrary, the plan was to expand my businesses. I was growing a brand. Creating a chain. Building an empire.

Sierra and I worked it out: he was to remain in Breckenridge (as the in-demand tattoo artist he was) and continue running our stores while I went to Vegas to set up more shops. But our ambitions didn't end there. We decided to also take a gamble with the Breckenridge stores by relocating both of them to the highest traffic area in town. It was a move that would triple our monthly rent but would position us as one of the prime retailers in the area.

We threw a going away party for me the night before I left town. When barely anyone showed up to it, though, I was pretty bummed. I had thought I had tons of friends, but I guess most really saw themselves more as acquaintances that frequented the same bars I did. I didn't know if they were all too drunk to remember to save the date or what, but I was pretty pissed to leave town on such a disappointing note. If anything, it really brought home the message that my time there was indeed over.

lock, stock, and barrel

> It's important when you're at a crossroads in your life to stop and take stock of what's working and what isn't. Then, to plan on ways you can pick up those pieces and move forward. In other words: Take Inventory.

After running my shops for a long while and trying every trick in the book, I came to realize that no matter how many themed "balls," cookouts, bowling leagues, and casino parties I threw together, in a town with only 2,000 year-round residents and a limited tourist trade, my earning potential was restricted—unless something changed. (This was before the internet had really taken off, and had I been able to set up Jimmy Vegas as an online store, the story may have been totally different.) After I crunched the numbers and met with Sierra, we decided that the only way to expand our business was to open more stores. It was both a decision and a direction I had been excited about.

It was the summer of 2001 when Mackenzie, my brother Matt, and I set off for new horizons. But in between settling down in Vegas and scoping out possible store locations there, I would return to Breck regularly to help with the construction on our new stores. Sierra and I had signed a three-year lease for them, and I wanted to be sure that everything was perfect.

Then September came, and tragedy struck.

fall of an empire

The terrorist attacks took the lives of about 3,000 Americans across New York City, Washington, DC, and western Pennsylvania while destroying the iconic skyscrapers known as the Twin Towers. The country was suddenly at war.

The disaster had far-reaching consequences.

Because the 9/11 attacks had been perpetrated through the hijacking of commercial domestic airliners, air travel came to a screeching halt. Tourism dropped to new lows all over the country and our sleepy little town relied heavily on the tourist trade. As a result, Breckenridge would see almost no visitors for a very, very long time. With our flow of income slowed to a trickle, our grand opening was more like a whimper than a bang. It was devastating. We gave it our all, managing to stay open for a few months in hopes that business would perk up after some time had passed. But nothing improved. We kept hemorrhaging money, and since we still owed suppliers and landlords, I had no choice but to close our stores just to stop the bleeding.

Had the 9/11 terrorist attacks never happened, this book might be a different one. But they did happen, and looking back, I can't help but notice all the times the universe seemed to be sending me signals or signs that it was time to put Independent Arts and Jimmy Vegas to bed. But because they had been my babies (and the source of some healthy cash flow), it took me a long time to accept those messages and move on. It would be a pattern I would repeat later. Sometimes it takes me a while to learn the lesson.

I had fallen to an all-time low. I was straddling two states, flat broke, and deep in debt. Sierra ended up footing our bills with the help of his tattoo income, and Double Down Enterprises was dissolved. The last months of our business partnership had been very stressful for us both, putting a lot of strain on the relationship and a great deal of resentment between us. It was a sad way to end what had been, for the most part, a very successful partnership and one hell of a run. I hated that Sierra had to pay off my share of our debt. (He hated it too!) But happily, I was able to pay him back in full a few years later when things improved for me.

Sierra ended up moving to San Diego, where he became the reputable and highly sought-after tattoo artist he is today. I am proud to say that 20 years on, he is still one of my best friends. When you meet and do business with quality individuals like Sierra, it's best to keep the books between you clear, and the bonds of friendship and mutual respect strong, even if you don't ever do business together again.

Relationships like that are something you can take to the bank.

With my dreams of being an entrepreneur and building a business empire now crushed, I found myself in a city with a population of over a million people, and with no source of income, no car, no connections, and no back-up plan.

what about you?

Have you ever been in the position that I found myself to be at the end of that chapter? It's called "rock bottom." Maybe you're there now and it's why you picked up this book.

This is not a coincidence.

When I found myself broke and unemployed in Las Vegas, it wasn't my first rock bottom experience. And it wouldn't be my last. But it was about to get very difficult. Not a time I like to look back on often.

But I share these experiences with you without shame or embarrassment because many of us have to go through rough times like these before we can make it to the top. And I think it's more helpful to let people know that in life you can sometimes be holding success in the palm of your hand one minute, only to watch it slip through your fingers the next.

Suddenly, I was back at square one. No, make that square minus one. I had gone backward and then some.

I have two words of advice for you, should you ever find yourself nearing a situation such as this one, or should you be in one now, or should you want to avoid falling into such a situation: Take Inventory!

If you stop and assess where you are now, you might build a battle plan for your business and may well avoid finding yourself in dire circumstances like I was.

For instance, if your business is slipping or can't seem to expand past a certain point, try comparing it to similar businesses—the competition. Is there a cap on how much money a business like yours can typically make? Is there a way you can reimagine it so that you can raise that ceiling

for yourself? What can you offer that the competition can't? If you don't have anything that sets you apart, can you think of something that might help you get an edge over your rivals?

Does the idea of figuring out something like that excite you? Then great, you probably still have some years left to expand your business.

But if the idea of retooling your business makes you cringe instead, it's probably time for something new. In these changing times, some types of businesses can quickly lose their relevance, especially if they rely too heavily on the popularity of a trend, if they are businesses that people can do themselves from home or are ones that can be automated. Is your business based around a trend that's in decline? Is it something an amateur can pick up easily and do from home? If it is, it may be time to move on to something else.

There are options, however. If your business is something someone can do at home, for instance, you can still work with it depending on what type of business you have. Take what Jennisse of JayLee Beauty has done, for instance. She creates video tutorials showing people how to use products she sells.

Another smart move that Jenn took was to create multiple streams of income by expanding on her brand. How can you expand your brand?

My tattoo parlor grew into a piercing/jewelry business and into a clothing business. Jenn's makeup tutorials grew into selling beauty products, a manicuring business, and then an apparel business. I know of a hair stylist who expanded from having her own salon to selling her own personalized brand of hair products, to creating a salon lighting company. (She also teaches hair coloring classes and writes a column on hair coloring for salon and hair product magazines.) As long as she is able to keep it up, she has different streams of income to keep her afloat. They all sprang from her original career and expertise—hair color—but if something were to happen to her hands or prevent her from physically going into work (like the pandemic lockdown) she has other avenues of income she can rely on.

Take inventory: what do you have in stock? What needs throwing out? What do you need more of? Is there something else you should start selling/providing?

Sadly, my businesses could not survive the economic crisis brought on by the 9/11 disaster. In much the same way, people were left to struggle during the global coronavirus pandemic of 2020. One of the reasons why my brand tanked was that my businesses were all tied together at one physical location at a time right before the Internet really exploded.

If I were to do it all now, I could continue to sell products online, of course. But that wasn't an option at that time. At that time, I was left flat broke—and broken—in Las Vegas.

chapter eight

riding the loser cruiser

"All great changes are preceded by chaos."

—Deepak Chopra

But I had had nothing before, so I wasn't exactly in unfamiliar territory. "Look on the bright side," I told myself. "At least you have a nice place to live." My first apartment in Vegas wasn't that great, but compared to the crap hole I had lived in Colorado, it was practically a resort. Not that I thought I would be able to keep it much longer since I barely had two dimes to rub together. "You'll get by," I told myself. "You always have."

I didn't realize how limiting that mindset was, because that was exactly what the universe ended up giving me: just enough to get by. Every. Single. Time.

Suddenly Mackenzie, Matt, and I all needed to find work in Vegas, stat. We also realized that we would need some kind of transportation to take us to those jobs—or even just to job interviews. So, broke-ass as we were, we got together and shelled out what must have been close to our last five hundred bucks for a piece of shit OldsmoBuick. But, realizing that with three of us we would still need at least one other mode of transportation and we certainly couldn't afford another car, we decided to use what little money we had left to buy an old moped too.

It was Mackenzie who found the ad for it in the paper, and I went with her to pick it up. That whole experience was bizarre. A little old lady was selling the moped. And when Mackenzie and I got to her trailer, we were both struck with an eerie feeling that didn't sit right with us. For one thing, there was an odd smell emanating from that dark and gloomy trailer, like the faint odor of death. And both Mackenzie and I felt strongly that there was something like an oppressive presence or spirit in the air. We later admitted to each other that we had half-expected the mother of Norman Bates to jump out at us or something—bloody knife in skeletal hand. The whole experience felt very haunting, and the memory of it still makes the hairs on the back of my neck stand up today.

Given that we both felt such foreboding, you'd think that Mackenzie and I would've said "Thanks, but no thanks" to buying the moped. But no, we went through with it. We were desperate. But a desperate attitude will not get you what you really want—just what you need to scrape by.

That's what we did over the next few weeks—we scraped by. By day we got around in our shitty car and haunted moped, and by night we stayed home, ate Taco Bell, and got shit-faced on cheap-ass liquor. In a way, it was like an echo of the old days when I was living in my car my first year in Breckenridge. But while the apartment was a step up from the van, living there while being broke as fuck was way worse. At least back when I lived in the van, I had found the lifestyle acceptable. No rent, no landlord—I felt nothing but freedom. But a decade had passed since. I had had a glimpse of the other side and wanted to go back to the kind of freedom that financial security had given me.

Things continued to go even further downhill when Mackenzie's moped was stolen from in front of our apartment (we actually suspected a neighbor but never got to prove it). Had we remembered how creepy the circumstances were when we bought the moped, we might have seen the theft as a good thing, but we were pretty devastated at the time. Not with just the moped, but with everything. I was so down, in fact, that I remember lying awake at night hearing military planes flying overhead and wishing more than once that one would just crash into our apartment and end it all.

Finally, Mackenzie found a job at The Bellagio as a massage therapist (which required her to use the crap mobile). Meanwhile, I pounded the pavement and hit up every store in the area for any job opportunity I could find. But because I had owned my own businesses for the last five years, all I kept hearing over and over again were two little words: "You're overqualified."

With our funds dwindling, I found myself growing more and more desperate as life seemed to be nothing more than a struggle to survive. But just when I felt the closest to giving up I've ever felt in my life, I took a job as a clerk at a gas station convenience store.

It was literally the only job I could get—a far cry from my flashy days as a business owner and man about town. Oh, and speaking of "town," did I mention that my gas station job was all the way across it? I not only had to take the bus to work—I first had to skateboard TO the bus stop since it was a long-ass distance from my apartment, and then from the next bus stop TO the gas station. At least I was able to put my old snowboarding muscles to good use.

Every day, as I took that loser cruiser to my "prestigious" new job, I sat in awe at just how far I'd fallen. It was extremely humbling to go from where I once was—with dreams of rising even higher—to where I now found myself: at the very bottom of the social and economic totem pole. What I felt went far deeper than being humbled, in fact, it was more like humiliation. It was like, no matter what I did, it would get taken away by someone, somewhere, somehow. I began to wonder what the point of it all was. I didn't understand then that success doesn't have to only come once and then that's it. That the road to success was actually a series of ups and downs. That it was all a part of the process. So, kids, listen up: when people tell you that the road to success only goes uphill—they're full of shit. I couldn't see it then, but even when I was riding the loser cruiser I was still on the road to victory.

Then I hit the jackpot—well, kind of. That is, I got lucky whenever someone else hit a jackpot in the convenience store. See, there were slot machines at the gas station where I worked (in Las Vegas slot machines are everywhere) and often, when someone won, they'd give me a nice tip from their winnings. Realizing that tips were where the money was, I began to cater to the regulars who I saw pumping their paychecks into the machines. On a good day I could make $200–$300 in tips. Things began looking up.

The owner of the convenience store also owned the gaming bar next door and I saw an opportunity. I took my tip money from the gas station and doubled down again, this time by attending bartending school. And I eventually talked the manager into letting me take the graveyard bartending position.

I began bouncing around to several of the bars owned by the company, always taking the graveyard shift. (You never really get used to graveyard hours though, so I was tired all night every night, and restless those times I was supposed to sleep during the day. It was a Bizarro World.) Even though the graveyard shift sucked, it still made me more money than selling condoms and 40s at the gas station, and I didn't feel like such a loser anymore. I did, however, often end up spending a lot of my money and off-time gambling at other bars (not on drinks—they were free). The only real downside—other than the weird hours—was dealing with drunk people all the time, but I had many years of experience in that department.

crossing the threshold

Once we were steadily and gainfully employed, Mackenzie and I decided to buy a house—which, by the way, in 2003, they would let anyone with a pulse and a pen do. Just the idea of becoming homeowners was exciting to us. Neither of us had ever owned a house before. The process of looking for the right place was fun—and nerve-wracking (especially since we had to take out a stated income loan). We really wanted to have a swimming pool and found the perfect little single story pool home for $169K. It was 1,500 square feet and located in an older area of Vegas called Spring Valley. It wasn't a great house, but it suited us just fine. We were thrilled and nervous at the same time when our offer was finally accepted. After all we'd been through, to be first time homeowners was a great feeling. I was quite proud of myself. Little did I know then that real estate would later become my calling. But first it would bite me in the ass.

Before that happened, though, home ownership inspired me to enter into another contract—and I proposed to Mackenzie.

It was a very "Las Vegas" proposal (yet understated in its way). We were outside the Bellagio Casino, at their restaurant where you can watch their beautiful and famous fountain shows. I chose my moment, and with Elvis Presley's "Viva Las Vegas" playing in the background, I took the ring out of my pocket, got down on one knee, and said those four little words. She said "yes" as the jets of water alongside us shimmied in time to the music.

After Mackenzie and I had been engaged for over a year and a half, our relationship fell on the rocks. But instead of taking inventory, I thought, I know! Let's put a Band-Aid on that shit and get married anyway! That will solve everything!

So, we threw a small, afternoon wedding at Angel Park Golf Course. There were only about 50 people—mostly family and friends—in attendance. Sierra was my best man. We had a reception and I danced with my mom to Lynyrd Skynyrd's "Simple Man." And that's what I vowed to be.

Shortly afterward, Mackenzie introduced me to a video called *The Secret*. It was all the rage at the time, and it heavily promoted the "Law of Attraction," "power of positive thinking," and "manifest your own destiny" schools of thought. I was fascinated by it. For one thing, it seemed to be more science-based than religion based. For another, it looked to be just what the doctor ordered. Like it could be the very thing that could make my marriage actually work. I was hopeful it would, anyway, and I gave it a few tries. I remember specifically trying to manifest improvements in my relationship with Mackenzie. I would lie on the grass in the park and try to visualize us the way we were in the beginning…

It didn't work. In fact, our relationship only got worse.

Next, tired of chasing after nickels and dimes all my life, I tried manifesting having more money. What happened? I got fired! Needless to say, I decided that either I wasn't doing this manifesting thing right, or *The Secret* was bullshit, and I gave up on the whole thing altogether.

Since I'd never been fired before, the whole thing came as quite a shock. But bars in Vegas make their money from gamers, and when gaming numbers are down, the owners try to find bartenders who have a nice, big following of gamblers. Or better yet, blonde hair and a big rack.

Unfortunately, I didn't quite meet those qualifications and the new manager replaced all of us existing bartenders with ladies that did match the above criteria. Still, as I said, it came as a shock because I was a model employee and all the customers loved me. And yet I could believe it because one, the new manager was a giant asshole, and two, I'd been getting a jealous vibe off of him ever since he'd first arrived and saw that I was a popular and established figure at the bar (which was what he wanted to be).

Even though I knew being fired was really about him being a giant ass-wipe as opposed to me doing anything to deserve it, I began feeling like a loser again. It was a blow because it was the first time I had ever been fired and my ego took a hit as a result. *Vegas is a cold, hard place*, I remember thinking at the time.

It actually took me several years of living in Vegas before I even liked it, to be honest. It was a huge culture shock to go from Breckenridge where everyone said "hi" to each other on the street and everyone had a common interest (skiing or snowboarding). In Vegas, the common interest was money, and that makes for a very cutthroat mentality. I actually hated Vegas at first because of this and that most certainly did not help with my mental mindset at the time.

ignoring the signs (again)

I took another graveyard bartending job at one of the video poker bars we frequented closer to home. I knew the staff, and they were excited to have me on board since they knew I was a good time and stayed up till 8:00 a.m. on a regular basis. I had worked there for about two years on the night of July 4, 2005, when I was held up at *fucking gunpoint*.

It was approaching 4:00 a.m. and I had about eight regulars left in the bar after a raucous evening of shots, jackpots, and extra loud classic rock—much busier than a typical night at that ungodly hour. Folks must have been feeling extra 'Merican, celebrating the birth of our country by drinking and gambling the night away. It was a lineup of the usual suspects for this particular establishment: Kelly, the blonde cocktail waitress who always tipped big when she won; Steve and Sheila, the on-again-off-again couple that occasionally got kicked out for arguing and who drank beyond normal human capacity; and of course, Frank, the bouncer from the strip club with his entourage of inexpensive women in tow. All the other employees and managers had called it a night and left yours truly to finish up the evening per usual.

It was a particularly good night for me as I'm quite sure I had cracked four digits in my tip bucket and players were still pumping C notes into the machines like they were going out of circulation. Suddenly, out of the corner of my eye, I see two young punks, hoodies pulled over their heads, stroll through the wide-open front door, flashing firearms, and demanding cash. I'm not gonna lie, it was pretty scary. Surreal even. The music, the laughter, and time itself seemed to come to a screeching halt. Everyone forked over their wallets as I handed over the cash behind the bar and, sadly, my tip money. The appropriate response, I'm told, when there's a handgun pointed at your face. No time to be a hero.

Fortunately, I was at least eight Jägermeister's deep, and I managed to keep my composure throughout the robbery. It was a traumatic experience to say the least. Thankfully, no one was shot. When the cops showed up, all that remained were several sobbing women and a trail of loose bills heading out toward the parking lot.

I couldn't sleep for several weeks. No exaggeration. I couldn't sleep for longer than an hour at a time without waking up in a cold sweat. As grateful as I was that no one died that night, I kept wondering, what if someone had pulled the trigger? What if that had been my last night on Earth? Or what if they came back and decided next time, I wouldn't be so lucky? I wouldn't have to worry about "next time," though, because I ended up getting fired soon after the incident took place.

The manager was pissed that the security cameras had not been running that night. But as I did not have access to the locked manager's office where the controls for the security cameras were, the cameras were not usually rolling during my shift unless he set them to do so. So basically, it was a bullshit excuse to fire me. He blamed the victim for the crime.

Because of this I—again—could have looked at my being fired as a favor from the universe, since I was now suffering from PTSD. The nightmares were the worst. I kept dreaming up different versions of the robbery where Mackenzie and I, or members of our families, ended up getting shot. Also, I could no longer perform my job with any kind of peace of mind, since I kept looking over my shoulder expecting the robbers to come back and "finish the job." But at the time, all I could think were things like, "Fired again! And for something that wasn't my fault? And now with the emotional baggage of trauma to boot? What's next, universe? You bitch!"

Had I paid attention to the signs, I might have understood that it was time to get out of bartending. But I only understood the message to be "get off the graveyard shift."

So that's what I did, and I took yet another bartending job at a new sushi and gaming bar where I was subsequently fired for a third straight time. This time after gaming numbers failed to reach their projected totals.

So, deciding that "job security" was clearly the problem, I applied for a bartending position at the Bellagio Casino— where Mackenzie worked and the site of my musical marriage proposal. The Bellagio is a union casino, which means that you have to really fuck up bad to get fired from there, so I figured I was pretty safe. Unfortunately, because it's a union casino, you also don't get to start off as a bartender right away or even as a barback.

So, down the ladder I slid as I became Las Vegas's newest graveyard "bar porter," a.k.a. night janitor. I was given the distinct honor of scrubbing bar mats, toilets, emptying trash, and cleaning floor drains each night/morning from 2:00 a.m. to 10:00 a.m. It was brutal. This was extremely humiliating as I recall being watched and snickered at by all the cute cocktail waitresses while I was on my knees holding a scrub brush with my arm down a nasty-ass black floor drain in the service well. It was the worst. But it was a turning point. Sure, it took me five years, three firings, an armed robbery, and my kneeling on the floor up to my elbow in crap for me to decide that I should be doing something else with my life, but everyone's got their limit, and I had just found mine.

what about you?

Sometimes we have to hit an all-time low before we can fix our situations and build our lives back to where we want them to be. Perhaps you are in that situation now and that's why you've picked up this book. I again invite you to examine your past and think about what's brought you to this point in your life.

This time I invite you to write down your work history: specifically, how long you've had each job, with what attitude (or emotional state) you began that job, and with what attitude/emotional state you ended it. Also write down whether you were fired or left on your own and why. This is for your eyes only, so be as honest as possible.

If you do this, you will find that an account of your professional history will help you to better see what you did right and where you went wrong. Again, all that self-judgment will only serve to paralyze you, and this book is all about moving beyond the fuck-ups of the past and moving into the future all the wiser for your experiences.

Next, I advise you to go over the list and use it to recall those days and the times that the universe gave you signs it was time to move on (that you ignored).

Again, this is not to feel bad—I don't when I look back, I laugh! Because now I've trained myself to see them, and when you go over your own similar experiences in the past, you will be training yourself to better recognize them in the future, too. Knowledge of past mistakes is still knowledge, and knowledge is power.

But I must warn that even with knowledge, we can continue to screw up if we fail to be completely honest with ourselves. And that's the hardest part. Because when we lie to ourselves it's often not even by conscious decision. And we end up making ourselves our own biggest obstacles to success.

For instance, because I know myself and how I prefer (and will always prefer) to be in charge of my own destiny, I told myself that was exactly what I was doing when I worked at all those bars. This was not true, of course. But because my self-esteem was low at the time, I convinced myself that it was, and that I was happy and was getting to do my own thing.

I see now that this lie was more out of self-protection than anything else. I had pushed down my dark and dangerous feelings of defeat, numbed them with alcohol, and was able to convince myself that I enjoyed work because I like people and get along with everyone. I even drank with my regulars (and most of them were doing just what I was doing, pretending to be happy and in charge of their own lives) and we all dwelt peacefully in that state of denial together.

I was able to keep this up for a long time too, because working the late shift meant I could tend the bar without a boss breathing down my neck, and it made me feel like I was the one in charge. Pretending to be my own boss gave me an excuse to not move beyond my situation and into a better one. But I kept getting fired by people who actually were my bosses—a truth I didn't want to see—for bullshit reasons. I kept getting knocked lower and lower until I had to be on my knees with a hand up a casino's ass before I could see the truth.

I actually thought about moving back to Colorado to try to get back some of the swagger I had there, because my tank was completely empty of that sort of thing here. But pride got in the way once again and I didn't want to go back to Breck with my tail between my legs. I had to find something else. But what?

"i feel you should fail a lot. you get better from failing."

An interview with Sierra Colt:
Renowned Tattoo Artist, Entrepreneur

Before he became the in-demand artist he is today, Sierra Colt was a professional snowboarder who won almost every competition he entered. This got him noticed and he was soon getting sponsorships by the truckload.

But then he heard the siren's call to become a tattoo artist.

Once he turned his attention to learning more about the art of tattooing, Sierra's snowboarding career suffered. First, he began to fall behind in his stats. Then he began to find it harder to keep up with the up-and-comers. Finally, he lost all his sponsorships. Before he knew it, Mr. Winning-Streak had to familiarize himself with failure as he struggled to create a whole new career for himself.

CP: Why would you leave something you were so good at for something you had to learn to do well? What made you switch gears?

S.C: Snowboarding is not something you can do professionally for a long period of time. Don't get me wrong, for a time I loved it. But sometimes you feel like you've gone as far as you're going to go with something and it's time to try something else.

I've always been an artist and I love tattoos. I also like to learn, and becoming a tattoo artist was sort of this dream I'd had in the back of my mind for a long time. Once I got started down that road, becoming a great tattoo artist became more exciting to me than being a great snowboarder. Actually, I wanted to be the best in the country!

Plus, I'm not afraid to fail. I think that's true of most snowboarders. You crash and burn a lot as you try to get better and better at the sport. And I think it's a good way to be. People should be taught to not be afraid of failure. In fact, I feel like you should fail a lot. You get better from failing. Absolutely.

CP: Your gamble paid off. You're a successful, in-demand, highly paid tattoo artist these days. Was it an easy transition from snowboarding to tattooing?

SC: There was a bit of a learning curve. If I'm going to be honest, some of my first tattoos were real pigs. When you first start learning, you're going to make some jagged lines, or you're going to make bad placement decisions in the design and stuff. But that stuff has to happen before you can get better. If you don't at least make that first line, then you can't make a second line, etc., etc.

In fact, probably the biggest thing I can share with your readers is that in art, your first piece will definitely not be your best. You're not just born with it. Well, some people are, but I'm not one of them. I had to learn everything. Most people do. When I look back now, I'm like, wow, I really had to do that to be able to do what I'm doing now.

I wasn't an overnight success. But most overnight successes have actually put in a lot of work behind the scenes: You know, grinding it out until four in the morning for three years straight to become that "overnight success." So, although some people might say I started doing well pretty quickly, the skill level I am at now actually took twenty years to get to.

But I've enjoyed the journey. I've never been the type to want to win something right away like the lottery or something. It would be nice for sure, but I don't want to just come out of the gate winning. I would rather have the experience of failing. I spent so many years learning the ins and outs and talking to other artists about how to design stuff and sharing secrets and tips and tricks and building up my knowledge of tattooing and skin and art. Now I'm here because I've spent all these years cementing my bricks of knowledge and foundations and failures. I couldn't have gotten here without failing.

CP: You really wouldn't want to win the lottery?

SC: It's way better to earn a million dollars than to win it. If I gave you a million dollars, you might blow it on some privileged shit, but if you *earn* that million dollars, you're proud of it. You have a story. Like, why did you earn it? How did you earn it? Who was with you? Who helped you? Who did you bring up with you? And you have a foundation of, "Well, I figured out how to do that. I spent a lot of time putting in the hard work of figuring out how to do that. And I know how I can do it again."

If somebody gives you a million dollars and you spend it all, well, then you've got to find somebody else to give you another million dollars because you don't know how to do it yourself. So, yeah, having the foundation you built yourself is way more satisfying. Even if you fail a lot along the way.

CP: So, what happens when you do fail? When all your plans and actions fall through, and things just don't work out?

SC: That's life, pretty much, isn't it? A lot of things that you hope for, try for, and think you can do, don't fully work out. And this can be any area of your life, be it love, business, or personal relationships. But I also think that more often than not, something better for you can come out of the failure. From it you can learn what it takes to actually be successful.

I am a big believer that when things don't work out, or when things you try do not succeed, that they are really just huge stepping stones. They are bricks that give your house a foundation. If you don't try these things, your house is made out of sticks, or out of old ideas that never solidify enough to be bricks. It's the failures that make the best bricks, or something really strong in the end.

When you're a snowboarder, to do well at the sport you really have to "go with the flow" and if anyone knows how to go with the flow, it's Sierra. By doing that, he was able to ride his snowboarding career over to Breckenridge, which carried him over to me, and led him to being professionally hired as a tattoo artist. This flowed into our creating a business partnership and then a friendship, and eventually brought him to California and to setting up his own tattoo business which is still going strong to this day. He sort of let nature take its course in helping him find success.

And in a way, that's what ended up happening to me. When I wasn't sure what career path to take next, I turned to a personal interest of mine, one that I had long practiced for fun but not for money, suddenly realizing what had been right in front of me the whole time: the chance to change my life around.

And change it did.

chapter nine

rock bottom and digging

"Rock bottom became the solid foundation on which I rebuilt my life."

— *J. K. Rowling*

I had dabbled in fitness when a friend of ours asked me to store his piece of equipment at my apartment back in Breckenridge some years earlier. It was one of those machines where you could do every kind of press and lift needed for weight training: Basically, an entire home gym in one monstrous contraption. My buddies and I would drink 40 ouncers of Mickey's and mess around on it in our free time at night with no clue what we were doing.

I had always thought myself to be rather skinny growing up, and hey, I figured that if I kept using this thing maybe

I could put on a little muscle and not be such a damn bean pole. Plus, it might be a good outlet for me since I wasn't getting the same release with snowboarding anymore.

I kept at it when I moved to Vegas and eventually purchased my own machine which I set up in my garage. I started working out daily, eventually saw results, and soon discovered my new thing. I decided to take some personal trainer courses and get a certification. And then I applied for—and got—a job at a 24 Hour Fitness gym as a personal trainer.

It was so cool to be able to make money doing something I was already doing out of enjoyment and personal drive. It was way better than those graveyard shift bartending jobs I kept getting fired from—where the universe itself had practically told me, "Get out of the bar business. You don't belong here." And it was great to be able to spend all my time in the gym, taking care of my clients and taking care of myself. Over time, fitness became not just a profession but a way of life, as I got more into it and less into drinking and partying.

You'd think all of those improvements in my life would have made me a better husband. And technically, they did. I was starting to live a much better lifestyle and was a healthier, happier man. But Mackenzie was still into the drinking and partying scene, so we began drifting apart all the more, widening the already present cracks in our relationship.

But I was ecstatic to be doing something different in an industry I was falling in love with. I would like to note here that I now realize why I loved fitness so much. It was the one thing I could control in a world that felt very much out of control to me. I could choose to exercise and eat clean foods and, with that, change my body. Nothing else I was doing allowed me to control the outcome more so than fitness.

Maybe it was this desire to control things—and my experience (and fond memories) of being an entrepreneur—but soon I found myself inspired to get out of someone else's gym and open my own business. I took most of my clients from the 24 Hour Fitness gym and became an independent trainer at another gym across town. It was successful and provided a steady income, but I could never seem to crack the $60K a year mark. Still, I was doing something I loved, and I was my own boss. Being my own boss is the best feeling in the world to me. I can't stand being told what to do or to have to come to work on someone else's schedule.

So, in an effort to bring in extra cash as a more respected personal trainer, and to challenge myself mentally and physically, I began to up my game by entering bodybuilding competitions. Over the years, I ended up competing in 10 Men's Physique competitions. I took 2nd, 3rd, 4th, and 5th place but never 1st. Truthfully, I found the whole arena to be disappointingly political, with the most deserving contestant not always taking home the prize. However, the overall experience was mostly a positive one. The process of getting ready for each competition took an incredible amount of mental training—along with the physical—because success in those competitions depends as much on one's mindset as on one's conditioning. Preparing for those shows taught me a great deal about myself and how far I was willing to push myself for something I wanted. Though I no longer compete, I'm proud of what I managed to achieve when I did, and I'm very grateful to have experienced that whole world. The lessons I learned have stayed with me to this day.

from partying ways to parting ways

Unfortunately, I did not put that same amount of work into strengthening my marriage, and it finally fell apart. After admitting to one another and ourselves that we were moving in different directions, Mackenzie and I sadly got a divorce. She will always hold a special place in my heart, as we went through a hell of a lot together. I still wish her nothing but the best. At the time, however, the divorce came as a severe blow. It was a truly crippling time for me emotionally. Yes, it had been mature of us to realize that we had drifted apart and wanted different things out of life, but it didn't make the breakup any easier.

I blamed myself for it all, too, because when I started getting into fitness and away from partying, I wanted very badly for Mackenzie to come along with me on the journey to a healthier, happier lifestyle. So, I began making comments to her about it all the time. As you can imagine, this did not go over well. She started resenting me. At the time, I was upset with her for not seeing that all my hard work was beneficial to her as well as me—hey, her husband was getting an upgrade! Meanwhile, she wasn't doing anything of similar value that I could "benefit" from. I transmitted my thoughts about this to her through various comments and complaints, and instead of motivating her I, of course, just ended up insulting her.

I didn't see then how it was one thing to try to exert control over my own life, but another thing altogether to try to control hers as well. I was doing to her the thing I most hated having others do to me. (No surprise—she also hated it.) I now know better that you need to let people live their own lives, and you can't—or shouldn't—force them to do anything that they don't want to do.

Back around that same time, our mortgage lender sent me a letter saying that I was eligible for their mortgage reduction program. This was great news! With the break-up, I was barely making ends meet with one income. The opportunity to pay half the amount I was used to paying a month could not have come at a better time. Jumping at the chance, I made sure to take all the necessary steps to complete all the paperwork and make this happen. Then I was instructed by our lender to not make my usual mortgage payments and instead to go ahead and start paying the new reduced amount while they were processing the paperwork. So, I did. For a year and a half. After which time I was told that I was not, in fact, eligible for the program and that I now owed all the past payments in full. WTF?

Of course, there was no way I could do that. Then, to add insult to injury, the real estate market crashed and suddenly I owed far more for the house than it was worth! It was bullshit. I would have no choice but to let the house go on a short sale. After which, having lost both my wife and my home in less than a year, I felt at my lowest point ever.

in the hole and out of the house

I had thought that by following and living out my passion I would find sustaining success. What people don't know is that the narrative is not always true. What is true is the real "secret." Following your passion does not mean you'll be coasting on wave after wave of success for the rest of your professional life. Shit will still happen and always will happen, whether you're sitting in a port-o-potty or on a toilet made of solid gold.

Too often, people believe that once you've found your "passion," you're somehow obligated to continue on that path for the rest of your life. That you are some kind of failure or fraud if you choose to let go of that "passion" and move on to something else. Again, I strongly disagree. I have found that following one's passion can lead to discovering another, or at least a new and different path. You should be open to seeing the signs in case something new and/or better opportunities crop up.

For instance, fitness is still a passion of mine to this day, but I am no longer a fitness trainer or a competitive bodybuilder. I don't feel a need to continue along either route, but I can appreciate that for the length of time that I did follow those paths, I found them enjoyable and educational and that they served me well. I still work out to this day, but no longer with the desperate desire of a man seeking to control some aspect of a life that was increasingly spinning out of control. Now I work out because I love the way it makes me feel, and I know when I do that I'm doing something good for myself and creating repercussions of health and strength that contribute to the improvement of every other area of my life.

Because real success should encompass every aspect of your life. If you're making the big bucks but you're a sucky husband or dad, or you're in poor health, or if you're just an asshole, you're only a half-assed success, which is to say, not a real success at all.

That's why I was feeling so down when I found myself without a wife, without a home, and deep in debt again.

I'd never felt more like a complete failure in my entire life. I slipped into a deep depression and was unable to laugh or smile for months.

Failure. Dead-beat. Has-been. These words tortured my brain 24 hours a day. I thought of the unthinkable.

what about you?

I've said it before: you don't have to follow your passion to become a success. But if you play your cards right, your career can *become* your passion.

I only began working out because I was storing that fitness machine for a friend of mine and thought, "What the hell? Let me give it a try." Once I got started, I began to enjoy the physical challenge. It was fun to keep pushing myself further and to build up my strength and stamina. And when I saw the results—the way exercise made me look and feel—it just made me want to work out more and more. Still, when I was first really getting into it, I was working out for my own personal improvement only and not with fitness as a career in mind at all. It just suddenly dawned on me one day that I could turn it into a possible career path.

What about you? Do you have a pastime that you would do—or that you currently indulge in—for free that you can turn into something more?

Let's think back on the lockdowns during the pandemic for instance. People took courses, read books, and watched tutorials all the while they were sheltering in place. A lot of people have become experts now at things they only had a passing knowledge of before because they wanted to pass the time during quarantine. Then again, a lot of other people binge-watched Netflix every day.

What about you? Are there any fun or interesting or educational things that you discovered during lockdown that could be turned into something that might financially support you? Or perhaps there is something you did for fun way before the quarantine that, again, wasn't necessarily a passion of yours but something that still interests you now—something you are interested in enough to look into further or learn more about and pursue in your free time. You might take a class in something (like a computer program or a certification or a college course) that opens up a whole world for you. You might even become so proficient in it that you end up teaching all you've learned to others. Cha-ching!

You might even have picked up something from those shows you binged on. You never know!

So, what are you into these days?

It could be that you enjoy conversations with others over a shared interest. Then why not start a podcast geared toward that very subject? (Especially if you can't find one that's already out there to suit your taste.)

Did you find yourself having fun creating interesting projects or worksheets for your children when you were forced to homeschool them? Why not try selling them online to other homeschoolers or teachers who could use the help?

Did you learn a new skill over lockdown? Maybe you can now create a product that you can sell or teach online? Have you learned how to make jewelry? Custom-decorate phone cases? Compose royalty-free music pieces? Make toe jam sculptures? Do you have expertise that you can teach on video and sell as a package of lessons? The possibilities are literally endless. The point is, they don't have to be your biggest passion in life in order for you to give them a try as a possible career path or at least as an extra stream of income.

Of course, I'm not saying *don't* follow your passion, either: some people really do have a passion and should at least try to follow it. If you fail, as I keep saying, it's not the end of the world, it will lead to something better, plus you'll have the satisfaction of knowing you've tried. Never trying to follow your passion is something you might regret for the rest of your life. Just don't get hung up on it. Some people really do succeed in following their passions—way beyond their imagination.

Take Brandon Stanton, for instance, a former bond trader from Chicago who, when he lost his job in 2010, decided to follow his dream of moving to New York and becoming a photographer. He even had a large art project in mind: to take photographic portraits of 10,000 New Yorkers and catalog them into a map of the city.

In the beginning he chose his subjects based on their looks. That is, they had to have something visually striking about them to make the photographs more arresting. Over time, however, he found himself drawn to more ordinary New Yorkers, like the ones he spotted standing on subway platforms or sitting on park benches. He started wondering about their personal lives and the stories they could share, and he began going up to them and asking permission to take their photos.

After initially encountering some resistance—people were distrustful of a stranger wanting to take their picture— Brandon honed his approach to make himself appear as non-threatening and sincere as possible. It worked, and soon people were spilling out their life stories to him. They even allowed him to record their interviews so that he could pull quotes from them to use as captions for the photos.

He posted those portraits weekly onto both his website and his Facebook page under the banner "Humans of New

York," and the popularity of this "online exhibit" soared to viral heights. His interviews and photographs inspired empathy from viewers, sparked three book deals, and got him inside Barack Obama's Oval Office. And with the financial support of fans, he has been able to travel internationally and take pictures of "Humans" in other cities and countries, share their stories, and successfully raise millions of dollars for charity causes. According to various sources (in a Google search) his own net worth has been estimated to be between $8 and $10 million dollars.

All this from taking pictures of people on the streets of New York.

And he may not have ever followed his dream and become the successful artist and impactful philanthropist that he is today had he not lost his job in the first place.

Perhaps one of the keys to Brandon's success was his positive attitude. He didn't let the loss of his job bring him down. Rather, he saw it as an opportunity to do something new. He also used a lot of that time to connect with other people. Obviously, he needed to do it for his work, but when he was doing it, he probably didn't immediately recognize the favor he was doing himself. His being able to make those human connections—constantly—is quite possibly what saved him from going down the rabbit hole of depression. In fact, being and sharing with his fellow "humans" is what became his trademark.

Quite different from where we last left me: alone, without a wife, without a home, and without a shred of hope.

"i got passed over...and then i got pissed off."

An Interview with James Epner:
Serial Entrepreneur, Internet Marketing Guru

Have you ever found yourself working for someone who didn't appreciate your contribution to the success of the company? Perhaps you find yourself in that position now.

When I left the gym to work as an independent fitness instructor, it was because that was—and is—my style. Independence. Freedom. Being my own boss, setting my own hours, and doing my own thing is just how I naturally prefer to work. However, I understand that for others, taking such a big step is more difficult to do. Scary, even. Like taking a leap into the unknown.

Perhaps you've never run your own business before. Becoming an entrepreneur can be risky, but with the right motivation and ability it can truly be your road to success. And if you are one of the many who are constantly overlooked for promotions or raises or you've even been fired from jobs you are doing well at, it's probably time for you to leave that bullshit behind and strike out on your own. Like James did below:

CP: How did it all begin for you, James?

JE: I was a fitness manager at the same 24-Hour Fitness gym that you originally worked at, and at the time, I was working real hard to move up within the company. My goal then was to impress the general manager of the area so that I could be offered the club manager position (which was the next position up) the next time it became available.

I really stepped it up and did my absolute best, exceeding even my own expectations. I mean, I had our team cold-selling fitness on the floor, giving out free sessions, and then doing such great jobs in those sessions that they turned them into $1,500 training sessions.

We did so well, in fact, that we smashed our goal for the month, which was $5,000, and made nearly three times as much: close to $15,000. Basically, 300% of our goal.

So, when the next club manager position opened up, I was pretty confident I'd get it. But, to my surprise, I got passed over.

Then I got pissed off.

I decided right then and there: *this is not a company that I want to be a part of anymore.*

Feeling under-appreciated and taken for granted, James decided to start a private personal training service at a different gym. There, he met a man who would change the trajectory of his life: an internet marketing expert named Kevin.

Kevin and James started training together and an exchange began. As James taught Kevin fitness, Kevin taught James the skills required to do internet marketing. When he later opened a CrossFit gym of his own, James then turned to those skills in order to attract clients. His self-marketing strategy proved very effective, and in time, James came to realize that if he could offer his marketing services to others, he could create a second business—and stream of income—for himself. So, he created a marketing program for non-competing gyms across the country and reached out to them—and it took off!

James started off making around $20,000 a month. Then his business quickly grew to *$200,000* a month. Then it grew to *$400,000* a month. And in fact, during their peak, the company made over *$2 million* in *a single* month.

As much as it sucks to have a bad boss and to be underappreciated—or even abused—at work, sometimes it's just the kick in the pants we need to make us move on toward our true destiny. James already had ambition and an entrepreneurial spirit within him. That was why he was able to motivate those under him to work the floor and surpass their monthly goal at the gym. But would James ever have branched out on his own if he hadn't been overlooked for a promotion? We can argue that it was his failure to get the job that started the chain events that would eventually lead James to far greater success than he had dreamed of.

I asked him about this.

> **CP: Do you think you would have met Kevin had you gotten the promotion you wanted at 24-Hour Fitness?**
>
> **J.E:** No, I would not have met this individual. I mean, *the worst thing that could have happened to me, I think I would have been to get the promotion that I was looking for*, because at some point it becomes a lot harder to quit. You know, when you're promoted, it's kind of like golden handcuffs. While in the end, I would have been somewhat successful, I would have been working 80 hours a week for something like $50,000 a year. And it gets harder and harder to quit the more and more you get promoted. So, for me, I never would have been able to start my own business and learn marketing the way I did without meeting Kevin.

CP: What advice would you give to someone who failed to achieve the dream or goal that they'd set for themselves, like you with the promotion?

JE: My advice would be to constantly learn new skills. Learn as much as you can, whether it's how to market or how to use technology or how to write code for computers or whatever it is.

For instance, every day, every month, I would take one of those online learning courses. You know, for $30 a month you can sign up at lynda.com and you can learn just about anything. You can really turn yourself into a Swiss Army knife of skill sets.

The reason I think that's so important is because *the more that you know and the more that you know how to do, the more ideas come to you. It's very difficult to see a good opportunity if you can't understand how to put it all together.* But if you've learned how to build a website, and how to get people to click on it, and if you know exactly how to build landing pages and write emails and all that—these things can be learned rather quickly with a couple of online courses—then all of a sudden, ideas start popping for you all the time. And you will see how and what it will take to get it to the finish line.

Then it's no longer just a dream. You'll have realistic, reachable goals where you can see exactly what you need to do to get an opportunity started. The more knowledge you have, the more you'll be able to connect dots and see something through to the end: it could be a very lucrative opportunity that you never would have seen had you not learned those skill sets.

Here is a clear case of someone being dealt a shitty hand, turning it around, and using it for fertilizer. James invested in himself, added to his skill set, and multiplied that initial investment by the millions. He didn't let another person's evaluation of his value stand in his way of seeing his true worth. It took some years to get there, but the return was truly worth it.

I, too, was able to turn the deep shit that threatened to bury me into good, enriching fertilizer. But I wouldn't be able to do it on my own. I would need to reach out and grasp in the dark for a helping hand.

chapter ten

live to fight another day

"Not everything that weighs you down is yours to carry."

—Anonymous

The only thing that stopped me from going through with it was the thought of my mother and how it would destroy her if I actually did it.[1] There's also this little thing called pride that gets in the way of your best-laid plans sometimes. So instead of hurting her like that, I decided to ask her to come live with me and help pay the rent for the small apartment I'd taken (since Mackenzie was staying in the house).

Mom drove right out and took a job as a chip runner at The Venetian Poker Room in the Venetian Casino. We lived together for about a year and a half.

---

1   If you or someone you know is at risk of suicide, please call the National Suicide Prevention Lifeline at 800-273-8255, text TALK to 741741 or visit SpeakingOfSuicide.com/resources for help.

It was humbling to have to ask her for help like that. Humbling in more ways than one. Here I was nearly 40 years old, having just gone through a divorce, about to lose my house and needing Mom's help just to pay the rent. But even so, it was better to do that than to devastate her by taking my own life. And I have to admit, it was healing to be around someone who loved me like that. Someone who not only didn't judge me, but was also willing to change her life temporarily to help me get back on my feet again. My mom would give her right leg if one of her kids needed it.

In fact, I advise anyone who has ever been in that sort of a position—close to losing all hope—to seek help immediately. And if you have people in your life that you know truly love you, then go to them, no matter how embarrassed you think it will make you feel. Think about it: anyone who's fallen into a pit needs someone else to at least throw down a rope ladder to help them out. Once you're standing in the sun again, you'll see that it was worth whatever mortification you felt reaching out. And you'll be in a position to help someone else out later should the opportunity arise (and it will).

After a year and a half, I was on my own again: Mackenzie moved out of the house, I moved back in, Mom returned to California. And finding myself feeling lonely once again, I decided this time the solution would be to find myself a companion. I wanted a dog, but I couldn't stand the thought of leaving the dog at home all day while I was out working. Cats are way more independent and don't need no stinkin' people around all the time—a bit like myself, I suppose. Maybe, I reasoned, a cat would provide me with the companionship I craved. I also hoped that caring for another living thing would take me out of my head and my problems and finally free me from my lingering funk.

I dropped by the local animal shelter and, after looking around, found a cat wobbling around inside her cage. She was a bit of an outcast—a cat who had been at the shelter longer than most because no one would adopt her—again, just like me. It turned out she had something called cerebellar hypoplasia, a condition in which the cerebellum of the brain fails to develop properly. The cerebellum is the portion of the brain that controls fine motor skills and coordination. The condition is not painful or contagious, but the cat had super-bad balance and couldn't even jump—I mean at *all*. She wasn't the kind of cat I'd had in mind to adopt when I first entered the shelter, but I figured no one else was going to want her, so I took her home.

I named her Baby. She was a very loving cat, albeit extremely uncoordinated. She would follow me around all day and sleep by my side at night. For a while there, she seemed like the only good thing I had in my life. If she was grateful to have a home with me, I was probably even more thankful to have her.

But I needed human companionship, too. And Jodie, a fellow personal trainer at the gym, thought she knew just the girl for me. One of her clients. A recently divorced woman named Jessica.

Jessica was very attractive. She was also a professional mixed martial arts fighter, so she was definitely physically fit and very assertive to boot. We hit it off, and after six months together, I moved in with her and her son. (I had to find a new place to live when I finally sold the house.) The arrangement worked for both of us at the time, though I don't believe either of us saw it as a "partner for life" situation, probably because we had both been burned by divorce.

Jessica had many great qualities but the one thing that bothered me about her was the tone she could sometimes take with people, including me. Being tough and strong-willed, she often got her point across by being confrontational or argumentative. I look back now and realize that she was a strong D personality type. And sometimes it downright pissed me off. On the other hand, I also really admired her tough-minded approach.

If you're unfamiliar, the D personality is from the DISC profile, which names Dominance, Influence, Steadiness, and Compliance as the main personality types. D's are characterized as decisive and dominant. They're risk takers and self-starters with high self-confidence who naturally assume leadership positions and expect others to look to them for direction. That was Jessica to a T.

As such, she was a real go-getter and had a very strong business sense to go with it (the wheels in her brain were always turning). And I absolutely learned a lot from her example.

In fact, when I now look back on our time together, I see it as a fruitful and formative season in my life that I wouldn't trade for anything. Learning to deal with challenging people can be a solid education. And with someone like Jessica, that education was more like working toward a business degree. They say you become like the people you spend time with, and I definitely became more and more like Jessica as time went on.

Jessica would often say that she felt like she was Good Luck Chuck in that every guy she'd ever dated started off as a nobody, and after their breakup would go on to become something great. I didn't understand what she meant at the time, but in retrospect I can see now that she had a tremendous impact on those men, and as a result made them better people. Not to mention better equipped for business. And better fighters.

She taught me the true value of believing in oneself and in taking the bull by the horns to get the job done. Our relationship didn't work out in the end, but hey, I give credit where it's due. And I truly believe that I would not be where I am today had I not studied at the "School of Jessica" and observed how she always went after what she wanted. How she refused to give up. How, if she fell, she got right back up again and moved on to the next thing.

Plus, she had legit high-dollar business experience. Before her divorce, she had helped her husband to build and run a multi-million-dollar fitness brand. This whet her appetite to achieve some kind of similar success again. So, we brainstormed ways we thought would allow us to achieve that together.

Then we hit on it. Since we were both into fitness, we decided we could combine our expertise and open up our own weight-loss clinic. We put together meal plans, sold a line of supplements, and set up a storefront to offer our personal training services. It was great to be back in business and have a real brick-and-mortar building to work out of again. Even if it was just a tiny storefront. We had hopes of branching out and maybe even creating a chain once the ball started rolling.

One snag, though, was that we had little-to-no marketing budget. So, with the exception of our rinky-dink, do-it-yourself website, we had minimal web presence. We hoped that our location, at least, would draw customers in. Yes, our place was tucked away and off to the side of the main foot traffic in the area, but we were sure we'd attract clients right off the street because we were situated near an "aesthetic" complex, where all the tanning, lipo/botox treatment, and hair/nail services could be found. And didn't we all cater to the same clientele? People who wanted to look their best?

We could not have been more wrong.

People who have cosmetic procedures and other beautifying services performed are not necessarily the same people who regularly go to the gym. In all those other places, the client passively receives a service while reading the latest issue of *Vogue*. At our weight-loss clinic, the client would have to work for their results—and work their asses off. They had to actively take part in their own improvement.

So, although we did manage to get a handful of clients every week, Jessica and I spent most days sitting inside our tiny workspace watching people and life pass us by.

We didn't last a year.

But our cloud of failure had a silver lining. Actually, more like a platinum one.

His name was George, and he was one of my weight-loss clients. He came in, bought a custom-made package, and began training with me three times a week. He was a good candidate for the program and he put in the work, so he made some good progress before Jessica and I had to close shop.

I gave George the bad news.

"What are you going to do now?" he asked me.

"I'm not really sure," I admitted.

"Well," he said and paused before asking me a question that no one had ever asked me before. "Have you ever thought about going into real estate?"

what about you?

Have you ever been so down that you've been tempted to give up? What is your mental state right now? Are you feeling at an emotional rock-bottom—enough to be having any thoughts of self-harm or suicide? If so, please put down this book and call the National Suicide Prevention number 1-800-273-8255 (or 911) and ask for help immediately.

That's what this last chapter was about: asking for and/or getting help when you need it.

We've all had times when we felt like complete shit about ourselves. I know, I've been there—on multiple occasions. In those moments it's hard to imagine a happier, healthier, and better future. Yet, if we hold on, those days *do* come.

Perhaps what I've learned most about myself each time I've gotten back up for another day of fighting is that I'm stronger than I knew. In fact, I believe that goes for all of us. *We are all stronger than we realize.*

Emotional strength is on a different level than physical strength. When we tap into that strength and power through the worst of times is when we are truly at our most badass. Yes, it's when we are most ashamed and filled with self-loathing and yet choose to survive that we can actually flip the script and become prouder of ourselves than we have ever been.

That's the good kind of pride: to accept, appreciate and love yourself on a deep and profound level. The bad kind of pride is the kind that sends stupid messages to your brain, like, "I'm better than my neighbor and therefore too smart to fail." Because when you do fail—and everyone does—that kind of pride will make you fall to pieces.

The bad kind of pride can also disguise itself as the good kind, like when you tell yourself, "I'm such a badass that I can do this by myself. I will rise from the ashes without help from anyone else." That's not how it works. What makes you a badass isn't that you survive your darkest moments without help from anyone. It's that you survive. Period. That you make it through to see another day.

It's the bad kind of pride that you have to swallow in order to ask for help.

Are there people in your life who you know will have your back no matter what?

I suggest you take some time now to think about those friends/loved ones/co-workers, etc., who you believe, based on your past experiences with them, would be willing or open to helping you out either emotionally or monetarily—or both—in times of need. It could be something practical, like helping you find a job; something more immediate, like providing you with food; or something healing, like taking the time to sit with you and listen to your problems. Whatever helps you best.

Write down the names of these people on a list and keep it handy or commit the names to memory. That way, if you are ever in a bad situation and feel like no one can help you, you can pull out your list and be reminded that there are possibilities. And don't forget to keep a look out for others who might be down and out to the point of despair, too. You might not be "there" at the moment, but someone else might be and you might be just the help they need.

What about companionship? When my wife and I broke up, I wasn't immediately ready for another romantic relationship, but I definitely needed loving companionship. I am fortunate to have a loving mother who came to my aid when I asked. But I also got myself a cat because I knew my obligation to take care of another living creature—especially one as helpless and rejected as Baby—could force me back onto my feet. If I couldn't do it for myself, I could do it for another that I was responsible for. You know what they say about "rescued" pets. They are the ones who really rescue you. And I have to agree. Baby paid me back for taking her in many times over with her loving companionship. And by putting her needs before my own, I was able to lift myself out of my state of complacency and self-pity and become more fully involved with life again.

What about you? Is there someone, a parent, spouse, child, or even pet, who needs your support or care even more than you need theirs?

Giving to others who are down and even worse off than you can actually help restore your self-esteem and help you to realize how truly "rich" you still are. It helped me to pull my own head out of my ass and get back to work and build a life for myself.

Love yourself—but with the good kind of pride, not the bad kind. If shit is fertilizer, love is Miracle Gro. Believe not that you're better or worse than the next guy, but that you're just as good, just as worthy to be loved, just as worthy to be helped, and just as capable of getting back on your feet. And remember that you don't have to do it alone.

I was a prideful, grown-ass man who had to call his mommy to help him pay the rent and to keep him from doing himself in. I have zero regrets about doing that. And my mother was more than happy to do good by her son. And what was the ultimate result of my deciding to live another day and the next and the next? Well, it took a little time, but my life has taken a major turn for the better. And boy am I glad to still be on this planet to enjoy it.

There's some awesome shit coming for you in your future. I just know it. Sometimes you have to wade through some awful crap first, just like I had to. But I found a diamond in mine: real estate. What will you find in yours?

"i hate to tell you this, but i think they've found their sucker."

An Interview with Brandon Roberts:
Founder/Owner of Signature Real Estate

BR: At the time I thought I had found my meal ticket.

I had been in the real estate business in Utah for a while when, in 2007, I had the opportunity to buy a region in Nevada for a real estate franchise sales company.

I closed on the region in October of that year, truly thinking I'd just made the deal that was going to be my answer to everything.

But I realized the horrible truth while on my first trip to Vegas—to meet with the existing franchises there—when I discovered that Vegas was going through one of its most dismal recessions ever. I could not have picked a worse time to open a real estate office. I should have done the research before signing on the dotted line. Still, I went forward with it because I had invested a ton of money into it already. But I realized that it was probably going to be a huge mistake while I was on a phone call with my business coach. (Yes, I had a business coach at the time.) I had moved away from family, friends, and everything I knew, only to meet with frustration. I asked him straight out, "What do you think? Can I even make any money at this?"

His answer? "I hate to tell you this, but I think they found their sucker."

And at that point, I knew that my plans weren't going to work out. That I wasn't going to go in the direction I had thought I was going to. But I resolved to make the best of it.

I worked really hard, opening six offices over a five-year period (although none of them were big). This depleted all my savings, as everything that I invested in (moneywise, timewise, and everything else-wise) had not worked out up to that point.

I made the decision to part ways with that company. This made for a sticky six-month period due to my contract with them. So, I very nearly had to live in my car.

Thanks to a mentor friend of mine, this didn't happen. Since he needed a house of his to be "short sold," he asked me to sell it and allowed me to live in it in the meantime.

While it was good to be living in a home, it wasn't my home. I used the time to look back on all the time and money I'd wasted and feel sorry for myself. I had hit rock bottom. Again.

CP: What other feelings did you have when you knew things were failing and crashing around you?

BR: The feeling of failure. What the hell am I going to do now? You know, like I said, I had no money, had no place to go. Yes, I could go back to Salt Lake, and I could probably move in with my mom until I got on my feet. But when I moved out when I was younger, my goal was to never have to go back home.

So that point was actually one of the scariest times in my life. But it was also one of the most instrumental. In fact, it was probably one of the best times in my life because it put me in a position to reflect and decide what I was going to do for the next chapter of my life.

Am I going to sell real estate? Am I going to move back to Salt Lake? At the time, it felt like the end of the world, but looking back on it now, I feel it really was quite a blessing.

Because that's when I made the decision to open Signature Real Estate Group, and I never really looked back. When I look at all the stuff that I went through during that five-year period of being down here by myself trying to make things work, and when I think about all the people I met and built relationships with, I realize it was all groundwork to create the opportunity to grow Signature to what it is today.

CP: Awesome. And then can you tell us a little bit about what you *did* end up achieving?

BR: When I bought the region and moved to Vegas, I actually had three real estate offices back in Salt Lake that I ended up selling. So, I lost those, too. I lost everything.

But now I've been able to rebuild three solid offices down here in Vegas that employ over 500 real estate agents in a model that has better retention. I also partially own a Signature real estate office in California. And I even opened an office in Salt Lake again—in the exact same building where I'd opened my first office there. In fact, the broker I hired for that location is the very first broker who hired me when I first got started!

CP: Great turnaround! What advice would you give to someone going through a failure or a perceived failure? Someone in the same place you were in years ago, feeling low about not being able to achieve their dream or their goal?

BR: Try to use this time to step back and evaluate. Everything is just a season. There's opportunity with everything, and it's not the end of the world. When one door closes, another door opens. I know it's not always easy, but periods like those can actually be tremendous opportunities when seen in the right light.

> You don't have to be a tycoon to have success. Look at me. I'm just an average guy. I go to work every day and do the little things. But if you stay consistent with the little things, then the big things can happen.

Brandon had dreams of building a little real estate empire and was even willing to make real sacrifices to reach his goals. He made grand gestures by leaving everything he knew (home, family, and friends) to make it happen. But he also made big mistakes, like not reading the market or doing the research, and this got him into some deep shit. But he was able to turn things around. And by forgoing the grand— and careless!—gestures of his past and opting instead to take smaller steps that were truer to himself, he found his way to success. He did not give up on his real estate dreams or choose another path, he just changed the way he forged it. Instead of building an empire, he grew a garden, through patient planting and what he considers being "ordinary"—and it's now a flourishing success, much like my own business.

But before I could get there, I had to start at the beginning and learn the ropes of real estate. Unfortunately, a few short weeks into my first job, I ended up hating it so much that I decided to quit.

chapter eleven

when one door closes

*"Most people miss opportunity because it's dressed in
overalls and looks like work."*
—Thomas Edison

George owned one of the largest mental health services
companies in Nevada. There were about 200 individuals
in his program, and they were housed in 50 or so rental
properties in the Las Vegas area. His problem was with the
property manager he had at the time. Nobody liked the guy,
including George. There were complaints from the tenants
that he was never around when they needed him. So, George
wanted me to replace him.

"Why don't you get your real estate license?" George
suggested. "Then *you* can be my property manager. You'd get
10 percent out of every rent check. Think it over."

I didn't have to think too long or too hard about it. My
weight-loss business was a bust and it was definitely time for

something new. Although I knew it would take me some time and effort to get the license, I figured it would be worth it in the end. "I'll do it."

What I didn't realize was that it would cost me a nice chunk of change, too—$2,000 to be exact. Money I didn't have. But you know how the saying goes, "You've got to spend money to make money." I figured that held true for this situation as well and jumped in, feet first. (When I go in, I go all in.) I drained my savings account and begged and borrowed the rest. Suddenly back in a classroom situation, Chris the straight-A student was back with a vengeance. I took my classes, aced my exams, and passed the tests with flying colors. In the end, I was a new man: a licensed real estate agent, ready to plunge into my new career.

And I had a guaranteed job waiting for me, too. Because George kept true to his word and immediately set me up as his new property manager.

With a mixture of relief and excitement, I settled into my new position and waited for the checks to start rolling in.

Then the phone rang.

And rang.

And rang.

And rang again.

I came to hate the job almost immediately. The damn tenants complained about *anything and everything*, all the time. As soon as I took care of one complaint, five others took its place. It didn't take me long to realize why the previous property manager was MIA all the time. (And I wondered if he really was, or if all the complaint-aholics just said he was.) Even though I was only managing three properties to begin with, the way they busted my ass all day—and night—it might as well have been 300. So, when I found out that I would eventually be expected to manage all 50 properties by myself, I quit.

Reading all of that, you might now be wondering why I then continued to pursue a career in real estate. Two reasons.

In the first place, I had invested too much time and money into getting my license to not at least *try* to make it work. Two grand was a shit ton of money for me at that time and I was NOT going to let it go to waste.

And in the second place, property management wasn't the only thing I could do with my license. There were other things I could try—like buying and selling.

When a door closes, open it again. It's a door, that's what they do.

But just as I was finding my footing in the world of real estate, the ground below me seemed to give way. Again.

when the cat's away

The first thing to give out from under me was my life with Baby. After her health took a downward turn, I ended up having to put my faithful companion to sleep. That loss hit me pretty hard.

The next thing to go was my relationship with Jessica.

"I have this friend," she said. "His girlfriend kicked him out of the house, and he needs a place to stay. So, I'm going to let him sleep on the couch."

It was all right with me. It was her house, her friend.

A few days later, Jessica announced that she and her "friend" were going to try to start a business together. This was also fine by me. I was just entering the world of real estate and I didn't have time for other entrepreneurial ventures. Besides, I knew how headstrong Jessica could be and how she was ever on the alert for business opportunities. It sounded to me like she was just doing her thing, as usual, while I was doing mine.

But then she began not coming to bed at night. And that *was* unusual. At the end of the day, instead of joining me in the bedroom to sleep, she would remain in the living room with her friend, working on their business. This awkwardness went on for about two weeks before I finally got the picture and decided to pack up my shit and go. It was time, and we both knew it.

A mutual friend of ours suggested I talk to her friend who was living alone. She referred me to Donovan, who didn't *need* to rent out a room, but since he had one to spare, took pity on me and let me into his home. He didn't know me and didn't have to do it, so it was really cool of him to welcome me like that.

What was even cooler was that although I was only renting that one room, I pretty much had full use of the entire house. Not that I utilized it, though. I was very respectful and kept to my room and an occasional trip to the kitchen to refuel. This was because Donovan worked nights and was asleep when I was awake. Ours became a "ships that pass in the night" kind of deal. This enabled me to use the house as an oasis of sorts, with time and space to reflect on my life—and to reconfigure my plans for the future. I owe Donavan a world of gratitude for he provided me with a much-needed safe harbor in the midst of yet another personal shitstorm.

And I ended up appreciating that harbor even more when, while scrolling through Facebook a mere two weeks after I moved out, I discovered that Jessica had changed her relationship status to "married."

I remember staring at the screen and thinking, *What the fuck?*

Yes, she had married her "friend" in a courthouse wedding.

The shock hit me pretty hard. I felt both kicked out of the house and kicked in the gut. She'd been with this guy the whole time I was there! It was hard for me to wrap my brain around it, let alone around the fact that because of it I had been reduced to living in a 10 x10 bedroom, furnished with only a full-sized bed, a borrowed desk, and an office chair—all of which I had financed for $350 from the local furniture store. Yes, I said "financed," as in, I had to take a loan from the furniture store for $350.

I nursed my wounds for about two weeks. But that was all it took. Because after those 14 days passed, I suddenly found myself feeling better than I had in a long time. I felt freer and more at peace with myself and with my life than I had in many, many years. It began to dawn on me that our break-up—and even how it happened—was all for the best. I could feel myself moving into a new phase in my life. And I just knew I was going to be okay: that my future was filled with infinite possibilities even. Or, at least, with the book *Infinite Possibilities* by Mike Dooley. Because after I read and studied that book, my life would be changed forever.

what about you?

Let's talk about Time and Space.

First: Have you ever been in a relationship that failed?

If you have, has enough time passed that you are able to look back on it and see the gifts it brought you?

While it's true that at the time I felt betrayed—not to mention devastated—when Jessica ran off with another guy and essentially kicked me to the curb, when I now think back on our time together, I am able to see past the hurt enough to appreciate the journey that it was. And I can honestly say that the pain was all worth it because it took me to where I needed to be next. In fact, it was a huge turning point in my life.

If you are still nursing the pain of a failed relationship, I suggest that instead of using up your energy on hating your ex or plotting revenge, you convert it into fuel to improve your own life and make yourself better and stronger through positive action. **After all, as much as you want it to be so, there is no guarantee that your significant other is going to love you for the rest of your natural life. The best thing to do then is to make sure that at least *you* love yourself for the rest of your life.**

This means self-care.

Although most people might have seen my living in a rinky-dink room (that I could barely afford) in a relative stranger's home while nearing my mid-life to be a huge fall from grace, I instead was able to see it as more of a fall *into* grace. Or a grace period. On the outside I appeared to be a struggling single man in a handkerchief-sized room. But looks can be deceiving. I was living in the lap of luxury, actually. The luxury of time and space. Most people don't

171

get that: a sanctuary free from the noise in which to sit and reflect on your past, refocus on your present, and rebuild yourself from the inside out to face your future.

So, what about you? What are ways you can take time and make space for yourself?

Keeping a journal can be one method of self-care. Hopefully, you've been writing in some kind of notebook while reading this book and taking notes. So many of us are busy to the point of being overwhelmed, but one method of keeping a journal is simply to write in it before you go to bed, to help you sift through the day's thoughts. So many of us are reading articles, playing video games, or catching up on social media before going to bed: we act like our phones are superglued to our hands. But in the same way that you can waste time on your phone, you can carve out 15 much more fruitful minutes to write in a journal. Especially if that helps you to think.

I don't have a great memory—I know, I've written a whole book of memories here, but my short-term memory and my memory for details could be a lot better. I find that writing things down is one of the quickest and easiest ways to not forget—at least it's a great help for me when I *do* forget things. It helps me to sit with my thoughts and in a small way recreate that "sanctuary space" I had at Donovan's. Without the time I had there to sit and reflect in silence and stillness, I would not have had the 180-degree turn that got me where I am today. That's why I recommend some form of recollection and reflection.

Meditation is another form of self-care, and there are many different ways in which to practice it. I personally love it. Some people prefer to meditate in silence. Others prefer musical accompaniment of some kind. Some practice contemplative prayer. Others do yoga. Some people go on weekend retreats in the country. Still others prefer the more cosmopolitan experience of a pampering spa day. These are all forms of self-care, and you should do the one that feels best to you. What's especially good about them all is that they mean taking time out for yourself.

Everybody needs time and space just for themselves, even the most social, goal-oriented person—maybe them, most of all, actually. We must all learn to be comfortable with just ourselves, just as we are, for company.

Self-care is kind of like spiritual, emotional, or mental hydration. Physically, the average human being is at least 60% water. This is why we cannot survive without water for more than three days. We need to keep ourselves replenished.

But, more than drinking a glass of water, taking the time to meditate or for some other form of self-care is like digging your own personal well to ensure that you'll always have water whenever you need it. Just think about the word, "well." If you want to be well, stay well, or do well, be sure to make "me" time.

It's what I discovered after doing it for myself: It cleared my head, sharpened my focus, and gave me the energy I needed to not only go forward, but to do so well that I could ultimately be called "well-off."

"some people will come into your life as blessings, others as lessons."

An Interview with Donovan McIntosh:
20-year Law Enforcement Veteran, Army Veteran, Entrepreneur

This book is not just about recovering from our business failures, but our relationship failures as well. This advice goes out to those readers who have gone through a breakup, are going through one right now, or who may go through one in the future. This one's for you. Success in both business and life can be yours—just hang in there. Listen to what my friend Donovan has to say about it.

DM: What really sticks out is my failed marriage, being separated from my wife for two years, and the misery and heartbreak that I experienced. And I recall praying and hoping that we would get back together. There were a lot of things that I wanted to change and a lot of things that I wanted to improve on. And I remember feeling guilty, because I felt like it's the man's job to determine the success or the failure of a relationship: It was a huge, huge failure for me.

And so, after getting divorced, I still prayed, and I still kind of wished that things would work out. Within months after our divorce was finalized, we would run into each other in church and talk. And then all the stars aligned and the next thing I know we go back to living together. I thought it was good. I thought it was gonna give me an opportunity to right some wrongs and try to do some things differently. So, I jumped back in with both feet. And unbeknownst to me, the feeling wasn't mutual.

I wound up wasting a lot of time, wasting a lot of money, and getting back into a failed relationship that ended miserably, worse than before. And it almost cost me my job, my livelihood, and thousands and thousands of dollars were wasted. It was definitely a lesson.

However, had I not gone through that experience, I wouldn't have the knowledge and the wherewithal to ask certain questions to determine the outcome of the relationship or to pretty much dictate the pace. You know, to not let someone else's needs or desires dictate the pace of the relationship. So, it actually set me up to be better for someone else.

It was a great learning lesson for me because I learned what I wanted. And I learned what I was not willing to accept. And I think in this particular situation I had thrown out all of my wants and desires and dreams and hopes and aspirations to accommodate someone else. And it backfired and wasted a lot of time. So, for me, it was a learning lesson and it made me a stronger man.

When it failed, it felt like true, true heartbreak. It wasn't like, you know, onto the next one. It was an actual heartbreak. It was depression. I went through multiple, multiple stages of the emotional roller coaster, where there was guilt, I blamed myself, I was angry; it took a long time for me to accept the fact that we didn't share a common goal. We didn't have each other's best interests at heart. And I was pretty much being used, so to speak.

The best way I can put it is that I went through all the hurtful stages of any emotional breakup, including depression. And the depression is what I'll say spawned a completely other side of me that I thought was put to rest.

I tried to fill that void, so to speak. And it wasn't necessarily with quality, it was with quantity. And, in turn, I wound up doing to other people what was done to me. So, it was a huge, huge learning lesson.

I wasn't in a position of being in a relationship. I was just trying to fill a void by any means necessary. And so, I created a revolving door with whatever and whoever, just to check a box. It was a dark time because, ultimately, all I wanted to do was be with the person that I wanted to be with for the rest of my life, and it didn't work. So out of anger and frustration and humility and disappointment, I took it out on the world.

CP: What benefit did you end up getting out of that, or end up achieving as a result of all those learning experiences and going through all that perceived failure?

DM: I learned a couple of things. Number one, I can be happy on my own. I don't need to juggle a squadron of females to be happy. It took me to a place where I needed to be happy on my own in order to make other people happy. And I wasn't really happy, so I disappointed a lot of people. So, it taught me to take care of and love myself before attempting to love others. That was the biggest lesson that I learned throughout that entire experience.

CP: Do you think you would have gotten to the point where you are now, where you've learned to love yourself, respect yourself, and live on your own if you had not gone through that relationship failure in the first place?

DM: Absolutely not. I think my head was so far up my ex-wife's behind that I couldn't see the forest for the trees.

I was just blinded by what I thought was true love and it wasn't. Probably I would have just hung in there to try to make it work as long as humanly possible.

CP: Do you think you're going to be happier as a result of the lessons you've learned than you would have been if that dream actually worked out?

DM: Yeah, I am happier now. I am happy now. I understand my self-worth, I love myself. I don't have to have a revolving door, and I don't need to have a squadron of females to define me, or my worth, or my love.

CP: What advice would you give to someone who may have gone through a similar situation or didn't achieve their dream or their goal? What advice would you give to them at the time it's happening?

DM: Never underestimate the power of prayer. Everything is in God's hands: some people will come into your life as lessons, and some people will come into your life as blessings. It's up to you to decide what type of person they are, which can ultimately decide the future you have with this person moving forward.

Just as Donovan was able to unwrap all the gifts that past relationships had given him, I, too, learned to be grateful for all that I learned through my (ultimately failed) relationship with Jessica. And once I accepted those lessons, I found it not only easier to look forward to my future, but to believe that the best was yet to come.

And I would not be disappointed.

chapter twelve

manifest destiny

"Thoughts become things, choose the good ones."
—*Mike Dooley*

"You never have to worry about money again."

That was the mantra I began telling myself daily after reading *Infinite Possibilities* by Mike Dooley. Yeah, it was another "manifest your own destiny" type book. But this one, for some reason, managed to resonate with me. Either the author explained it better than the others had, or I just happened to be in the right state of mind to receive the message. I had tried earnestly years earlier after watching *The Secret* but had given up. This time was different. I found this particular book to be written in a more relatable way—for my personality at least.

For instance, I really liked the way the author had provided actionable steps to take. I've always been the kind of person who can think of new ways of doing things, but I can also be a great student when I feel the teacher knows more than I do. And that's exactly what I found Dooley to be: a damn good teacher.

In fact, he was kind of like a spiritual fitness instructor. If you follow an exercise regimen correctly, you get results. So, I approached the instructions in the text the same way I would a workout. And, in time, I found myself better able to focus and put into practice the conscious creation of my reality. I saw real changes start to happen for me. In the end, whether you choose to believe in the law of attraction or conscious creation is totally up to you, but I think we can all agree that you do have to take responsibility for your own future.

Taking responsibility for the events and outcomes in your own life is both immensely rewarding and—at the same time—monstrously terrifying. Nobody wants to be the one to blame if things go tits up. — I get it.

So, to avoid this white-knuckle situation, many otherwise upstanding individuals will choose victim mentality. Victim mentality is a hell-of-a-lot less risky than responsibility, and you're never the one held liable if things don't work out.

Playing the victim justifies and validates your failures. It's like a "Get Out of Jail Free" card for the weak. It's far easier to play the victim because it relieves you of the duty of creating the life you really want. "It's not my fault that I can't get ahead. I would, but my circumstances suck." "I would have the life of my dreams, but I can't because my boss is an asshole." "I only steal from people because society has done me wrong." Victims will even assemble to further corroborate each other's horrible luck and misfortunes.

Taking full responsibility, on the other hand, empowers you to do what's otherwise impossible.

Your perception is your reality and if you perceive yourself to be a victim, then that is exactly what you will be—a victim. A victim of circumstance, unable to control or even partially influence the events and outcomes of your life. At the absolute mercy of others and your surroundings. A fallen leaf on the raging river of life.

If on the other hand you perceive yourself to be in control of—and most importantly responsible for—your destiny, then you, my friend, most certainly will be. It's some scary-ass shit. But you know what? It's the most fulfilling and gratifying feeling in the world.

So how do you take control of your life? By not *trying* to control it.

"Everything you can imagine is real."—*Pablo Picasso*

loosen your grip

Real estate has afforded me many things over the years. The ability to travel, to make my own schedule, to work from the comfort of home. Freedom.

It has also afforded me something that I had never considered before: insight into the minds of thousands of people, and in particular, an insight into their beliefs surrounding money. Especially large amounts of it. For most folks, buying or selling a house is one of (if not the) biggest financial moves they will ever make. Definitely top five.

But thanks to my work, I get an up close and personal look at the values and beliefs about the almighty dollar that people have carried with them their entire lives. It's an insight others don't often experience.

And you know what I've discovered? Most people are holding onto what money they have so tight that their hands are about to cramp up. They chase nickels and dimes down the street like a dog pursuing a parked car and fail to see the big picture. I have found that this happens for one of two reasons:

They honestly believe that money is hard to come by and that they must claw and scratch for every last penny—or—there is an unrelenting need to be in control of money and/or get one over on the other guy.

Instead of sending out the message, "Money flows to me with abundance," they are telling the universe, "Money is hard to come by" and worse, "I can only hold on to a little bit at a time." And regardless of the message they send out, the universe will always respond (in the words of my buddy Rich Lopp): "Yes, that is true. Here's some more evidence to support that."

It's counterintuitive I know, but that's exactly how it works.

Remember, you get back what you put out, so if needing to squeeze every last nickel out of someone just to make yourself feel better is what you're into, then I have news for you friend, you will always be in that position. Needing to gouge, needing to claw, and needing to fight for every last dollar—for the rest of your life. Sound like fun?

If you think, act, and play at a minor league level, you're never going to get called up to the bigs. It's that simple.

It's far more productive in the long run to take the perspective that "Money comes easily to me," and "I don't have to worry about money," etc. Even if it isn't necessarily true for you at the moment. Can you see the difference?

This reminds me of a professional poker player I know. He says that to do well in no-limit poker you almost have to have a *calculated disregard* for money. "Scared money doesn't make money," they say.

This is not to say that you should be reckless and throw caution to the wind with your financial decisions. They should be taken seriously. But for the love of God, loosen your damn grip on money. It's not going anywhere, and there's plenty of it to go around.

why the rich get richer

You've undoubtedly heard the expression "the poor get poorer, and the rich get richer," but what does it mean and why is that so? For most of my life I assumed it meant either you had to already have a bunch of money in order to make any, or that the system was somehow rigged and stacked against me. In other words, it was an excuse, and further validation as to why I didn't have any.

Now, however, after 50+ years of life experience and after having worked with thousands of individuals in large financial transactions over the years, I know the real meaning. I've discovered, not surprisingly, that the less money someone has, the more fearful they are about opening their wallet. The more they have, the more they're inclined to open it. There are exceptions to this, of course, but, generally speaking, this is painfully true. I've also come to the realization that the less money someone has, the more they feel they are entitled to it.

"Well, no shit Chris, that makes sense, of course you have to hold on to your money tighter when you don't have much," I hear you saying.

Sure. It makes sense, but not in the way you might think. The "Financial Death Grip," is actually the cause of, and not the solution to, one's financial worries. Every time you haggle with someone over a $20 widget on OfferUp, every time you scan a 25-cent coupon, and every time you stress incessantly about upcoming bills, you're telling the universe that money is hard to come by and that you don't have enough of it. Your relationship with money needs an attitude adjustment, stat.

Now, I'm by no means suggesting you throw hundred dollar bills out the window of your car or burn them at the strip club in a display of affluence. But if you can just loosen the stranglehold you keep on your cash, that will start to tell the universe that you're okay. Small, seemingly insignificant acts—like paying for someone else's coffee at the drive-through—are not only acts of selflessness but statements that you have plenty to go around. Try tipping 50% the next time you get good service at dinner, or try giving that homeless person $10, even if you know he's gonna buy vodka with it.

These acts will begin to change your own thoughts—and eventually your beliefs—about the supposed scarcity of cash, and once you believe something to be true, it usually is. It may seem wild to you that just changing what you think, and therefore believe, could possibly influence what happens in your experience, but it's the straight-up truth.

when the student is ready

So, I replaced my usual thoughts and worries about not being able to pay the rent on time, for example, with pictures of myself living the confident and financially stable life of my dreams. I meditated day and night on these visions and willed myself to believe that they would happen for me. I was finally ready to be responsible for whatever happened next. And "next" meant taking action.

It was soon afterward that a gentleman named CJ came into the brokerage where I worked and gave a one-day class on online marketing. A bunch of us took his class, but I was the only one who really took his lessons to heart. I followed everything he taught to the letter and applied each and every lesson to my practice—just as I had with the information I found in *Infinite Possibilities*. There was a ton of work involved, mind you, because there were so many time-consuming steps I needed to take in order to build up my online presence. But CJ had promised that the sooner we completed the steps, the sooner success would be ours. And he turned out to be 100% correct.

I was the only one of the agents that day who fully took and followed through with all his advice. And it showed. Because after a while, customers began finding me online, and my business took off. I was suddenly the top selling realtor in my brokerage.

Finally feeling in control of my life, I decided to take a gamble on another business venture, and I launched my own private-label supplement line. It was something I'd had in mind to do since my weight-loss company days and could finally put into motion now that I was making some bank again. I sank $10,000 into the idea and called the label "Living Proof Labs." Then I got 200 bottles of each formulation and sold...maybe five.

This was a big setback, similar to previous failures I'd had in the past, but with a difference this time: the loss didn't break me. In fact, I was doing so well with my real estate business that I decided to let Living Proof go. I just didn't have the time to put the same amount of attention and dedication into it as I was putting into my primary business.

Sometimes, when I think back on it now, I can't help but wonder, had I been able to stick to it and really build up a good web presence for Living Proof, would it be doing well today? I was proud of the quality of the product, but regretfully ended up having to throw it all out because I had no place to store it.

Even though Living Proof was a bust, I don't regret giving the supplement business a try. In business, we can be faced with some hard decisions. I had to choose between something that had great potential but needed work to achieve that potential, and something else that was already working and doing very well for me. It made better sense to choose that which was working, even if it meant giving up on a dream. I made the right call for me.

swipe right

But when I wasn't working (which was hardly ever), I tried to get back into the dating scene. I tried out a few dating apps and saw a few different women for a few months, but it turned out to be a lot of work, too—another full-time job, actually. And, after a while, I found that trying to keep up communication with various people through an assortment of apps had become an exhausting juggling act. Tired of the chore that the casual dating scene had become, I decided to delete all the apps but one: Bumble. It was an app where the woman had to be the first to send a message once the two of you had matched. It took a lot of the pressure off the man and empowered the woman at the same time. I liked that.

When I came across her profile, I swiped right immediately. She was a young blonde, petite and fit. Definitely eye-catching. I was interested from the get-go. I hoped the feeling would be mutual and that I'd hear from her as soon as possible.

When she got back to me, I was very excited but a little disappointed that she didn't want to meet in person right away. She insisted instead that we first only text each other through the app. As she was a burlesque dancer and waitress, however, I understood her need to be wary of strange men. After texting back and forth for a while, we graduated to FaceTime conversations. After about three of those, she finally agreed to meet in person.

Our first date was at the Green Valley Ranch Casino for pizza, drinks, and a little video poker. The more we talked, the more we found out what we had in common, and the more we hit it off. I found Erin even more beautiful in person, as well as surprisingly funny and really sharp. She was a triple threat.

But it was when she cooked a gourmet meal for me within the first week that we started dating that I knew for sure: after all my years in Las Vegas, I had finally hit the jackpot.

When things started getting more serious between us, I suggested that we move in together. She lived in Henderson, which was about a 30-minute drive for me, and my having to constantly drive back and forth between our places was getting old: Since we were together all the time, it made much more sense for us to live under one roof. So, we found an apartment in Las Vegas and signed the lease. It was the first place that was neither hers nor mine but ours.

It was awful.

It was our upstairs neighbors. They were incredibly noisy. It sounded like they were dancing all the time. And I don't mean to music on the radio. I mean it sounded like they, legit, had a stripper pole installed in their apartment and were practicing pole dancing routines. It sounded like a pack of rabid hyenas had been permitted to occupy the apartment directly above us.

On top of all that, there were a lot of rules and regulations in our apartment complex—when and where to throw out the garbage, pick up your mail, etc.—rules about everything *but* pole dancing and hyenas. We didn't let the year run out on our lease before we left. Then I *bought* a place.

When I settled into my new home and my happy life with my new girlfriend, I couldn't help but feel grateful for all the shit that had come before, because the result of it all was my now being truly where I wanted to be, with the person I wanted to be with, doing work I not only enjoyed doing but did well.

I have learned something from every success and every failure. In some ways, to be honest, I have learned even more from the failures than the successes. Things like: failure itself is always just temporary and there is always some good to be found wrapped up inside of it. For instance, my former girlfriend essentially forcing me to move out was a sucky thing to have happened. But in reality, it was one of the best things that had ever happened. That little 10 x10 room in which I ended up became my regeneration chamber. It was there that I spent an incubation period, reflecting upon and reordering my life until I could be reborn as a new man. On top of that, Donovan, who so kindly allowed me the space to do this, has remained one of my best friends to this day and was my best man when Erin and I married in 2018.

Because of the mutual respect my wife and I have for each other, our marriage developed into a true partnership. We did (and still do) everything together—even entered fitness competitions. The three times we did proved to be very challenging experiences. It takes several months to prepare for a show, and that training period is extremely taxing on the body as well as the mind. Tempers run short as the effects of restricted calories and exhaustion take over. What was great though was how each time we went through it only strengthened our relationship. Like going into battle together.

On the home front, she continued working full-time as a burlesque dancer and cocktail server. She knew five different dance routines and would sometimes step in for lead dancers when they needed a night off. When one of the headliners she sometimes subbed for went on maternity leave, Erin asked to be the woman's regular substitute for the time she was away. She knew the routine well, had been a loyal and hardworking employee, and deserved the spot. However, they told her no, that she could have only one show a week or nothing. She chose nothing.

I was proud of her for knowing what she wanted and for taking her shot. I was even prouder of her for knowing her own worth and respecting herself enough to walk away at the right time.

I wasn't worried when she quit, because I was making more than enough to support the two of us. Plus, I knew I was with a smart woman who would be able to find something else in short order. But then it occurred to me: burlesque dancing paid so little in comparison to what I did for a living. And she'd picked up a lot from watching me work from home. So, I turned to her, and I asked the same question that had been asked of me a few years earlier:

"Have you ever thought about real estate?"

what about you?

As you can see, I am a big believer in manifesting your own success. But it took me years to get here. I had to realize that manifesting isn't about magic. It's about intention. And it's about *doing the work.*

Oh, yes, I did a lot of picturing a future of financial security. We're talking hardcore envisioning—because I really wanted it. But you can't just demand what you want from the universe without lifting a finger to bring it upon yourself. The universe is not a genie. It is a co-operator.

If you want a beautiful mansion, you should take care of the humble home you have first. It shows the universe you are a good caretaker, and you can then be rewarded with more because you have proven you can be trusted with it.

As much as I envisioned my success, I also did everything I could do to make more money—like taking that online marketing class and working my ass off 10–12 hours a day. The class was offered to everyone, but I was the only one that paid attention. I followed every word of advice the teacher gave. I didn't throw away or waste any of the knowledge he imparted, and it worked out very well. I did the work. I did it believing that if I followed his instruction, I could make myself financially secure to the point of never having to worry about money again. And then it happened.

I also did the work when it came to looking for my life partner. At first, I was using a slew of dating apps and playing the field to the point of nauseum. I thought that was "doing the work" and showing the universe I was looking hard for "the one." But most of those dates just resulted in casual hookups. When I felt it was time to seriously settle down, I figured out it was best to get rid of all apps but the one. And that's when I met my future wife. And she made me work for it as evidenced by the many FaceTime dates we had before meeting in person. And that's how it should be with anything you really want. When things come too easy or are handed to you on a silver platter, you take them for granted. When there is more input and effort on your part, you feel accomplished and proud when you succeed. It's so much more worth it.

So, what about you?

What are the goals you would like to manifest for yourself? What desires are you willing to put in the effort of both envisioning and physically bringing about into your reality?

Is there a course in a subject that could perhaps add to your skillset and make you a more valued employee where you work—skills that could result in more sales for your company, or an increased income for yourself and perhaps even a promotion? Or, if you work for yourself, is there an online marketing, accounting, or salesmanship class you can take and then apply toward improving and increasing your business? I found it very empowering to learn how to market myself—as good for self-esteem as it was for the wallet. Those are the kinds of profits you can take to the bank! My advice to you is to research (and if you can, apply for) classes that are available either online or at your local library or college.

Then there are times when you do all the work and still fail to get what you wanted, like when Erin didn't get the spot in the burlesque show she'd worked so hard for. It sucks to be unappreciated. And in times like those, it's usually best to leave, like she did, with your self-respect intact. It's good to know your own worth and to protect your assets (or your own ass) rather than allow some asshole boss to take a big chunk out of it.

> **In a nutshell, "When you know you are worth more than they are willing to pay, sometimes you gotta walk away."**

Erin did just that. And it would be one of the smartest moves she would ever make.

chapter thirteen

letting go

"Often when you think you are at the end of something, you're at the beginning of something else."

—*Fred Rogers*

She dove in headfirst.

I taught her everything I knew. She followed every piece of advice I gave her, and her business went from zero to $150,000 in one year.

She used to make $120 a night as a dancer.

Needless to say, Erin turned out to be a real natural at real estate. She was even named Rookie of the Year at the company we worked for.

Watching her shine made me feel incredibly proud. Then my entrepreneurial light switched on again.

Why don't I create my own team, I thought, and make her my partner?

And that's exactly what we did: we set up a home office and became The Patrick Group (ChrisPatrickRealty.com)

Erin now manages our growing team and has been integral to its growth and success. It helps that she loves being her own boss as much as I love being mine (I told you we have a lot in common), and that she was able to pick up the real estate business as well as she did. She teaches and coaches the other agents on our team as well as agents for our parent brokerage in other offices and around the country.

It's been eight years now since I got my license, and we've sold well over $100 million in real estate. We've even invested in the parent company of our real estate brokerage.

And we've invested in homes of our own: that is, Erin and I have bought and sold six homes of our own in the last four years. My proudest moment came, however, when I was able to purchase a home for Mom. I actually bought Mom's house before I bought my own. It was a dream I'd had for as long as I can remember, and to hand her the keys to her very own home was surreal. She cried her eyes out.

Being so solvent sometimes makes it hard for me to believe that it was not even a decade ago that I was struggling to make the rent each month. I mean, the worry used to consume my days and nights. But no more. I haven't stressed over money since locking in my mantra and deciding to take responsibility for my future. And I truly believe I owe a lot to those visualization exercises. Had I not diligently practiced envisioning a future filled with ever-growing success, I don't believe I would ever have managed to achieve the level of financial and personal success that I have today.

dreams developed/dreams dashed

That's why I was so grateful when, in 2019, I got a chance to meet Mike Dooley, the man whose teachings changed my life. Erin and I attended a workshop he had in Reno and signed up for the VIP roundtable discussion with him after the event. It was a full circle moment for me as I got to tell him—and everyone there—how he changed my life. I think this was the first and maybe the only time my wife has seen me tear up a little. It was very emotional for me.

There's a famous saying—more like a warning—"Don't meet your heroes." This is because the people we put on pedestals often end up being so disappointing in real life. Real dicks, even. But not Mike. He was so cool when we met him. We actually ran into him in the elevator at the hotel on our way to the conference. We got to talking and he turned out to be a super down-to-earth and personable dude.

Erin and I still practice manifestation exercises and believe that it's thanks to them that we were recently able to move into a brand new, million-dollar dream house. It's a real beauty and custom built for us, so it's everything we could want out of a home. It's put an end to our moving days, and it's the place where we are putting down our roots to raise a family

Because that was the next dream we were working on making into a reality: parenthood. By now, as you've already guessed, Erin, my amazing wife and partner in everything, is the same Erin whose interview about the adoption process you read about in Chapter 6. Her story is actually our story, and it continues here.

After deciding that adoption was the best route to achieving our dream, we began going through the domestic infant adoption process. We were matched with an expectant mother around the same time I began to work on this book, so I anticipated being able to write about the successful adoption of our baby by the time I reached the end. But I had just begun writing when once again, the shit hit the fan.

After months of building a relationship with the birth mother who had agreed to place her child with us and taking her to check-ups, appointments, and dinner, Erin discovered through social media that our "match" was not intending to place the child for adoption at all. It was a scam. A scam for money and emotional support. This heartbreaking discovery hit us both hard, but even more for Erin than me. I'd never seen her so crushed or defeated. She would confess to me later that it had made her feel as though there had been a death in the family.

As we dealt with our disappointment and feelings of betrayal, I returned to working on this book. In doing so, I found myself reflecting all the more on my life's journey up until the present. The setback with the baby, I realized, was just another shitty roadblock on our road to happiness: It would and could be surmounted, just as all the previous shitty roadblocks had been before it. Despite my sadness and frustration, I was also consoled by the realization that at least this time I hadn't lost my home or my job, and I wasn't starved for either food or companionship. Best of all, I had Erin. Together, I knew we could weather any storm. Her presence made a huge difference in my life. Whatever happened to me in the future, I knew that as long as she was by my side, I could call myself a success. She wasn't just my wife, she was my partner, and the most loving friend a guy could ask for.

She would also make an excellent mother. That's why I hated seeing her fall into such a deep depression after having her dreams smashed to bits. She couldn't even rally her spirits on Thanksgiving Day, since she had anticipated our spending it with our new baby, Jameson—the name we had picked for our child whether it was a boy or a girl. The day after the holiday, we sat down together for a heart-to-heart and agreed that wallowing in negative feelings was not going to get us what we wanted. "We will get the baby that's meant for us," I insisted. "But in order for that to happen, we first have to let go of the baby that wasn't meant for us." After this dark and painful conversation, she agreed and promised to put the past behind her and start fresh in the morning.

The very next day, the phone rang.

what about you?

Is it time for your "second act?"

Have you been working hard at something—even something that you've done well at for the last 10-15-20 years but have yet to get as far with as you have wanted or had planned to do?

Is it perhaps time to try something new?

How do you know when it's time to let go of a dream?

Yes, Erin was able to quit her job at the burlesque show because I was making enough to cover the two of us. Still, that didn't make her decision an easy one. Dancing and entertaining was what she knew. She kept herself in shape for it. She loved learning her routines and knowing when she had nailed her performances. It gave her a sense of pride, a sense of satisfaction to know her shit and to do it well.

And, basically, it was the only career she had ever known.

So how did she know when it was time to leave that dream behind? What prompted her to draw the line?

Self-respect.

Erin saw that she wasn't going to get a fair chance to do a job she knew she could do well. She also understood that if she didn't stand up for herself in that instance, she would be signaling to the powers that be that they could walk all over her. She decided she wasn't going to let them control her career or make her feel badly about herself. So, she walked.

It was one of the smartest moves she ever made (besides marrying me, of course ;-)).

When she walked away from the first half of her professional life, she walked into a new beginning. She left herself open to trying something new and completely different. And that receptivity allowed her to give real estate a try—something she turned out to be not only good at, but great at!

What about you? Are you in a place where your profession is no longer serving you? How are you feeling about yourself in the career you are currently in? After reading this far in the book, are you feeling invigorated about boosting your career and envisioning greater future success in the line of work you are in? Are you inspired to go after your dream more than you ever had? Or are you feeling let down by your dream? Beat down by "the man?" Have you fallen out of love with your career?

Erin had no idea that she'd be any good at real estate, but she'd been watching me for a while. And like I said, she was naturally smart. She and I both thought that with the proper training she could do it. And we were right!

Do a self-esteem check. Your dream job or career really shouldn't be making you feel like shit about yourself. If it does, it's not your dream job.

And just as you are stronger than you know, you are smarter than you know. It could be that, given the chance, you can learn to do a job you've never even considered before and do it better than some people who've been doing it for years—a better job than the one you are doing now that you have lost love for. The key is to find it, and then really apply yourself to learning it.

Be open.

That means keep your eyes, your ears, and your heart open to new possibilities. When you make a move that reinforces your own self-respect, you're definitely moving in the right direction and priming yourself for better things.

Sit and think. Do you need to move on from the job or career you have now? Do you feel good about yourself doing it?

Is there someone you know—a friend, a spouse, or another family member—in a line of business that you have never considered before that you could consider now? Why not give it a go? If that friend or family member is an expert in their field and willing to show you the ropes *and* it's something that could build your self-esteem (and your bank account), it could be worth a shot.

Erin took her shot—and it landed her in the tax bracket of her dreams. With that, and feeling secure in her marriage to me, she realized it was finally possible to adopt and support a child. But when that dream was snatched out of our hands, she held onto the memory of that lost adoption as if that had been her one and only chance at happiness. Her unwillingness to let go took a toll on her mental health and even put a strain on our marriage.

Once she learned to let it go, just as she had her dancing career, she unblocked herself from receiving the good that was coming to her.

I am a big believer that once we accept not getting what we want, and release our stranglehold on it, we actually end up not only finally getting what we want but, often, getting something much, much better.

Do you want to achieve your dreams but only in the way you want? Or are you open to the possibility of receiving much, much more?

Some people call this "letting go." You might see it more as showing the universe you are ready for the next phase in your life. Others say it's living with intention.

Why not write down your intention? Something like:

"I am ready to receive the life of my dreams in its best possible form and in the most perfect timing."

Put this someplace where you can see it every day. Maybe on a door you walk through every day so you can read it and say it to yourself each time you step through. Whenever you say it, mean it in your heart, making a real effort to let go of what you think your success is *supposed* to look like, while strongly believing that it will happen for you. Then go about your business. Do the work. Treat yourself and others with respect. And don't forget self-care. Then watch the magic happen.

For Erin and me, it happened *the day after* she released the heavy burdens of feeling betrayed and disappointed and replaced them with the very real intention to instead be at peace and move forward.

At three o'clock that afternoon, our social worker called.

"you have to let the situation breathe"

An interview with Erin Patrick, Part 2:

The story of how the universe gifted us with our daughter is a wild—and wonderful—ride.

CP: When we left off, you and I had come to an agreement about how to move past the deep disappointment of the failed adoption.

EP: Yes. You and I learned a lot about each other during that difficult time. I think going through something that painful can either truly make or break you as a couple, and to be honest, it brought us almost to our breaking point. Not that we were going to get divorced or anything, but it was really, really, really trying. But once we finally opened up and said the things that we knew could hurt the other and tried not to take them too personally, it was the greatest thing that we could have ever done—for each other, for our marriage, for our situation.

Also, I realized that ever since we were first matched up with the expectant mother so early in her pregnancy, I got really caught up in preparing for the baby. I was going to every appointment, buying this and that for the baby at every and any opportunity. My entire world became this baby. And it was like I forgot you in all this! It was definitely not on purpose. But I just kind of went "tunnel vision."

And even though we were super-disappointed and saddened by the failed adoption because you really wanted the baby too, you were also thinking, "Oh, my gosh, did I just lose my wife too?" So, we had to have some really, really hard talks that were uncomfortable. But I'm grateful for them—and even very, very grateful that the match ended up failing because it brought us through probably one of the worst times in our life as a couple. And it gave us the opportunity to be vulnerable and honest with each other and to communicate, even though it was difficult and painful. And the biggest thing I learned was how much support I have in you, even though I already knew you were an amazing human being.

We have an even stronger bond because of what we went through together. You were even able to pull me out of my depression.

CP: So, there was a gift in the failure. Do you think we would have gotten to this point in our relationship had you not gone through that failure?

EP: It's hard to say. There will always be challenges to a couple's relationship, really. But I don't think we would have this deep of a connection this early in our marriage had we not gone through this horrific tragedy together, no.

CP: What advice would you give to someone that has gone through something similarly tragic or a traumatic event? Or who has had their dream crushed?

EP: So, it's interesting when people ask that question, because it's so much easier to see once you've come out of it, and so hard to see when you're still going through it and you feel like your world is ending. But the advice that I would give to anybody, whether they're going through an adoption situation, or something is not going the way they want it to, is this:

You have to let the situation breathe. It's easier said than done—believe me, I know—but you have to just let go and let God or whatever you believe in take control. Everything is being set up for you so that you can achieve everything that you want. And if you continue thinking about your goal in the most positive of ways and basically tell yourself, "This is going to happen, I know that this is going to happen," and keep manifesting your dreams, it *will* happen, and sooner than you think.

But if instead you continue to think negative thoughts, like, "Why is this not happening for me? Why can't I get what I want?" All that the universe can hear is "not" and "can't" and "don't" and "won't," and you will be blocking all the "yeses," "cans," and "wills" from getting to you.

So, the takeaway is: try not to focus on the negative—especially in tough situations. Try to stay as positive as you can and think of things other than, "Why isn't my dream coming true?" If you sit everyday with your thoughts, it can be a good thing—*if* you are focusing on the positive. But if you are dwelling on the negative, it's only going to break you in the end.

When our baby match started off so well, I really thought it was our time. That we had been through enough in our efforts to become parents. But God said, "No. You haven't been through what you need to yet. You have to go through this pain to get to exactly what you want. You'll see."

CP: And did you?

EP: Yes! On Saturday, the very next day after I had promised to put my disappointment behind me and to forge on, we got a phone call. Apparently, just a few hours before I had made my resolution, a little girl had been born at a local hospital—to a woman who hadn't even known she was pregnant! She wanted to place her child for adoption as soon as possible. So, if we wanted her, they told us, we could have a daughter as soon as Monday!

CP: The timing of it all was kind of ironic, wasn't it?

EP: Well, ironic is an interesting word for it. It was certainly humbling. It makes me laugh. Do I think if I had gotten over the failed adoption sooner our situation would have ended differently? Probably not, but it really was a beautiful turn of events, I will say that. And it's like the universe was waiting for me just to let go. And once I finally did, it said, "Okay, now I'm gonna give you everything that you wanted."

chapter fourteen

jackpot

"All our dreams can come true, if we have the courage
to pursue them."
—*Walt Disney*

It was the Saturday after Thanksgiving when we got the most
exciting news of our married life.

Miss Ann, our social worker, called to tell us that there
had been a baby "stork drop" in Las Vegas. In the adoption
world, a "stork drop" is when a birth mother who has just
had a child at the hospital wants to relinquish her rights.
Miss Ann went on to say that we were the first potential
adoptive parents she had called and that the baby could be
ours as soon as Monday if we were interested.

We were interested!

Erin and I are now the proud parents of a baby girl. The
story of her birth is fascinating and really seems to confirm
that she came into the world to be with us.

The birth mother was from out of town but was in Vegas visiting with her parents for Thanksgiving. Throughout her pregnancy she never had morning sickness, never showed a baby bump, and she had no idea she was even pregnant! Then, on Thanksgiving Day, she was suddenly in labor.

Unable to recognize what the severe abdominal pains she was experiencing were, she panicked and feared for her life. Her equally panicked parents drove her to the local Quick Care, where she was seen immediately.

Her water broke a few minutes later when she was standing in the middle of a crowded elevator. Again, the young mother-to-be panicked, unsure if she had wet herself or was even dying. But the doctor inspected her and told her she was "crowning."

"What does that even mean?" the young woman asked.

"It means you're pregnant and you're having a baby right now!" she was told. And the baby was delivered right there and immediately whisked away for an examination.

After the infant was determined to be premature, she was taken by ambulance to the local hospital where they have the best NICU in Vegas. There, the doctors referred to the baby as a "fetus" since they didn't know if she would live.

Once the baby was stabilized, however, the hospital informed the mother that the child was out of danger but still needed to be kept there for several days for evaluation. It was then that the birth mother decided she would place the baby for adoption and the call was made to our social worker.

It was all so perfect for us: The baby was born right in Las Vegas, which meant we didn't have to immediately fly to some other state and stay there for several days. A stork drop meant that we didn't have to wait and wonder for months on end whether the placement would go through and risk another heartbreaking scam. It was a girl (which we wanted). And it was a closed adoption, which meant that the mother didn't want visitation.

To have all these criteria met in this way is extremely rare in the adoption world.

When we went to meet the birth mother and her parents, things were a little awkward at first, because we were, essentially, complete strangers to one another. The situation was made all the weirder by our having to wear masks due to the pandemic.

So, there we were, all blinking at each other over our masks when Erin opened her arms a little and asked the birth mother, "Are you okay with a hug?"

And she answered, "Yes, please, give me a hug."

Erin told me later that she felt like the birth mother had really needed it, and I had to agree. The warm bonding moment between them seemed to break the ice, and soon we were all talking and discovering interesting similarities between us.

Like, how the birth mother's mother (our daughter's grandmother) is in real estate, just like us. Or that the reason why they were in Las Vegas was not just for Thanksgiving, but to celebrate the grand opening of the burlesque show their *other* daughter was performing in. So, the baby's aunt was a dancer just like Erin had been for 20 years.

Also weird was how the birth mother's father (our daughter's grandfather) has the middle name James and is occasionally called "Jameson"—the name we had chosen for our child—by his friends when he's had a little too much to drink!

It really was like our soon-to-be-adopted baby was actually our own flesh and blood.

When Erin asked the birth mother privately if she was *sure* she wanted to give up the baby—a little afraid to begin to allow herself to love the baby only to have it snatched away from her again—the birth mother assured her that she did. She even confessed that had she known she was pregnant months prior to the surprise delivery, she would have terminated the pregnancy.

The birth mother went on to say that, initially, she'd been so traumatized by the surprise labor experience that she had questioned why God had allowed her to go through such a terrifying ordeal. She had also been deeply worried about how she was expected to care for a child that she was so totally unprepared to look after.

But once she began considering adoption as an option, she started feeling better about the whole thing. Excited even. And instead of seeing the child as a burden, she began to see how the child could be a blessing for a couple who really wanted to be parents. And once she finally got to meet us and see how happy we were to get the baby, she was thrilled about her choice. Seeing our joy and knowing she had made it possible, made all the pain she'd endured worth it.

When we were finally able to hold the baby, we pulled down our masks and Jameson's grandmother exclaimed, "She looks just like you guys! I don't know how that's possible, but she is your child! She looks just like you two!"

Erin beamed at me. "God's hands were all over this," she said. "It's just a miracle."

As I write from the beautiful home I share with my incredible wife and amazing daughter, I can honestly say that I have everything I want. But in getting here, I have learned that things rarely work out exactly as planned. There's always some little twist or turn—and sometimes a full blown shitshow of a failure. The important thing is to make sure to pivot or adjust accordingly. Knowing ahead of time that things will probably work out differently than you had anticipated helps when they do go south. The path you choose might turn to the left or right or it might hit a complete dead end. No matter what happens, though, you absolutely must start down a new path, or you will miss the opportunities that come to you. Opportunity definitely favors the brave.

Look, nobody wants shit to happen, but it does happen. It always happens, and to everyone—even the richest, the most famous, and the most powerful people. No one can live a perfect life. Ever. People who say they do are straight-up lying to you and to themselves. It's what they want you to believe. People like that are not interested in helping others achieve the same level of success—or higher—than they have because then it would expose their lies, their brokenness, and their shame. They would rather that you think of them as perfect and untouchable because it makes them feel better about themselves, even if it leaves you in misery.

But I don't want to be like those who can't or won't show their true selves to others. I want to be myself. And that means not denying every failure or shitty experience I've had. Instead, it means sharing it all with you to show you that if all this crap could happen to me and I still made it, so can you. The key again is to not be defeated by defeat. And to not let the shit make you *feel* like shit!

I made it through—and now I have it made.

For this to be true for you as well, my advice is to always be open to any path that the universe opens to you. Definitely chase your dreams, but if along the way you are shown a new path, stop and take a good hard look at it for consideration. Many times, you may be on the path toward your dream for the sole purpose of finding a new path that can lead you to even greater heights. Sometimes our dreams can be far more limiting than the opportunities the universe really wants to show us. If, instead, you are open to the possibilities, your chances of success are multiplied tenfold. Impossible, you say? Impossible is just an opinion, and you know what they say about those.

So, this is where my story ends—for the purposes of this book, anyway. And the ending is not only happy, but also true.

Now it's your turn. What about you? How can you get your happy ending?

I hope that in reading my story and reflecting on your own personal journey through the questions and exercises provided for you on the WAY pages, you have been inspired to make a success out of your own life—however that looks and feels to you.

I also hope that you can view yourself, your life experiences, and the world around you in a new light. That you can now laugh at and learn from past mistakes. That you look back

jackpot

and discover the hidden treasures buried deep in your old fuck-ups and disasters. And I hope you also know not to give up when things seem their worst. It *will* get better. It may take some time, but trust me, it will. And when it does, sometimes it can get *insanely* better!

Most of all, don't let the shitstorms drag you down. And the next time you fail to get what you want, trust, believe, and get ready to receive. Because the universe is going to give you exactly what you need.

acknowledgments

This book would not have been possible without the loving support and understanding of my amazing wife Erin. Thank you for standing beside me and believing in me throughout this journey. You're an incredible partner, mother and wife. I love you.

I would also like to give a huge shout out and a big fist bump to the rock stars that were kind enough to share their stories with me in the writing of this book. It's not easy to admit your failures to the world, and without them this book would have been a lot smaller. Please check them out and connect with them as well.

erin patrick
https://www.instagram.com/erinbpatricklv/

++

jennisse
JayLeeBeauty.com
Instagram.com/JennisseMakeup

++

rich lopp
https://www.youtube.com/RichLopp
https://www.facebook.com/UniversalTarotZone

sierra colt
bearcattattoo.com
Instagram @sierracolt
SierraColt.com

++

james epner
https://www.linkedin.com/in/james-epner/

++

brandon boberts
BrandonRoberts.com

++

donavan mcintosh
https://www.instagram.com/donavan_unleashed/
https://www.facebook.com/donavan.mcintosh.9

Last but certainly not least, thank you for your purchase and reading of Disasters to Dreams: A Gritty Guide to Finding Success in the Face of Failure. This book was written for you, and I would love to hear your thoughts about it.

What's next? Consider leaving a review! You can leave a review on Amazon, Goodreads or on the book's product page on the retailer's website where you purchased this book. Show some love and pay that shit forward!

Also consider sharing your thoughts about the book on your own Facebook, Instagram, or Twitter. Feel free to tag me and let's build our circle of success.

Don't miss the latest updates and more at ChrisPatrick. net. There you can sign up for my email newsletter, read my blog posts and follow me on social media. Let's continue the discussion!

Need help buying or selling a house in YOUR AREA? We have an amazing network of agents all over the country. Connect with us at ChrisPatrickRealty.com to find out more!

With my sincere gratitude for your support, remember, sometimes getting your ass kicked makes you better.

- Chris Patrick

Made in the USA
Las Vegas, NV
05 May 2022

48435739R20132